Memoirs of an Art Dealer 2

Memoirs of an Art Dealer 2

G. Blair Laing

G. Blair Laing

McClelland and Stewart

The Canadian Publishers
McClelland and Stewart Limited
25 Hollinger Road
Toronto M4B 3G2

Trade edition printed and bound
in Hong Kong by Leefung-Asco Printers Limited

Limited edition bound in Canada

CANADIAN CATALOGUING IN PUBLICATION DATA

Laing, G. Blair, 1911-
Memoirs of an art dealer

Includes index.
ISBN 0-7710-4571-9 (v. 2)

1. Laing, G. Blair, 1911-   2. Art dealers —
Canada — Biography. 3. Painting, Canadian — History.
I. Title.

N8660.L35A25   338.7'617'0924   C79-094522-3

Contents

Preface

I was surprised and delighted with the reception of my first book, *Memoirs of an Art Dealer*. After several years of writing and research I was able to fulfil my commitment to finish it, and when it was finally published I felt that a dream had come true. As stated on the first pages of that book, my original idea was to produce a work on the art of my favourite Canadian painter, James Wilson Morrice, with suitable colour plates (a book I am still hoping to write), but found myself instead telling the story of my own life as an art dealer.

I soon discovered that writing a book of memoirs involved some deep inner searching into memories of the past. I also found that recalling events that happened a long time ago triggered a mental process that in a curious but positive way added to my own self-knowledge, and for some unexplained reason brought a greater meaning to my life. Of course my memories were sharpened by consulting the firm's old records and hundreds of other relevant documents, books, and photographic material.

As strictly a novice writer I went through many periods of trial and error while working on the manuscript and all sorts of self-doubts plagued me from the start. Lorne Pierce, the legendary editor of the Ryerson Press, and one of Canada's early cultural nationalists, was a selfless, magnificent man. He left a lasting influence on my life. Regarding the aspirations of budding writers he had this little tip: "You will always be more effective if you say it in your own way." But even doing it your own way takes a lot of practice and hard work.

Canadian art has had so much publicity in recent years that many people were curious to learn more about the art dealer's world. But *Memoirs of an Art Dealer* turned out to be much more successful than I had ever thought possible. There were not only many

1 James W. Morrice *Léa in the Garden, Bois-le-Roi* c.1900

reviews, but, more important, there was a warm and sustained response from the public, which continues to this very day. I have savoured many good experiences in life through the years but none, I believe, has given me more personal satisfaction and a sense of real fulfilment than the completion of that book. Also it was a pleasant diversion for a few weeks before Christmas, 1979, to visit neighbourhood bookshops and watch *Memoirs* gradually disappear from the counters and shelves.

The success of the book, and the enthusiastic reponses I received and still receive more than three years after its publication, encouraged me to write further of my experiences as an art dealer, highlighting stories about other artists and personalities I have known throughout the years.

Memoirs of an Art Dealer 2

2   Paul Kane   *Indians Salmon Fishing, Kettle Falls, Fort Colvile*   c.1846

1
Governor Simpson's Missing Paul Kanes

Of all our nineteenth-century Canadian artists, Paul Kane has made the greatest contribution to our Canadian heritage. While he proudly referred to himself as a native Canadian, he was actually born in Ireland, in 1810. His parents, along with their young family, immigrated to York, Canada West, from Ireland about 1818. Muddy York, as the capital was then nicknamed, became Toronto in 1834. By 1818 York was beginning to grow and had a population of about 1,200 people. The earliest settlers were United Empire Loyalists, who fled from the United States in the aftermath of the American Revolution. The good prospects in Upper Canada continued to attract immigrants from England, Scotland, and Ireland, including the Kanes. Paul Kane's Anglo-Irish background blended smoothly into the strict puritanical mold of little English-speaking York during his growing-up years. Serious, and single-minded as a youth, he had no time for practical jokes or frivolities, nor, in his journal, do I find him displaying much humour.

Young Kane received a few years of education at the district grammar school; education was then not considered of prime importance and generally ended at an early age for both boys and girls in pioneer York. As a youth he apprenticed in a local furniture factory as a decorative painter and designer.

Self-taught, but with the natural talent of one born with artistic genius, Kane decided to try earning a living from portrait painting, first in Cobourg, and later, from 1836 to 1840, he worked as an itinerant portraitist travelling in the eastern and southern United States. Like the Methodist preacher travelling from pulpit to pulpit, the itinerant painter journeying from town to town was a common figure. It could not have been an easy existence for Kane, as commissions were few and far between and competition keen. However, in Mobile, Alabama, he did finally receive several much needed commissions. He was now able to achieve his cherished ambition of a trip to Europe for intensive study.

Kane, who was endowed with great natural drive, desperately wanted to learn more about his craft and he made the trip on his own in 1841. There is no evidence that he attended art school or studied under any painting professor while in Europe; he believed in diligent practice and self-discipline. Even if he could have afforded the luxury of studying at art schools and with drawing masters, he somehow preferred to work on his own, although sometimes he took walking tours with art student friends. His main source of income at this time was probably the sale of Old Master copies, which he executed with felicity and care. His father may also have made him small loans on occasion during these crucial years.

Kane returned to the United States from London early in 1843, and by April of the same year, he went back to Mobile where he accepted portrait commissions. When Kane returned to Toronto in the spring of 1845, this time for good, he was now eager and ready to fulfil his youthful dreams of painting the North American Indians, their abodes, and their way of life. They were the source of his inspiration and stirred his imagination. Paul Kane's field sketches of the Indians he encountered on his great 1846-1848 western trip are probably the finest painting of native peoples ever made over the entire North American continent.

We tend to think of Tom Thomson and his painter friends as artist pioneers of the north. By 1915 Thomson was working his painting magic in Algonquin Park and three years later J.E.H. Mac-Donald transformed Algoma autumn subjects into pictures of haunting beauty. Consider then the daring and resourcefulness of Paul Kane pitching his tent among the Indians on Manitoulin Island in 1845, nearly three-quarters of a century before Thomson and his friends visited the same north country. Kane, Krieghoff, Tom Thomson and J.E.H. MacDonald share the distinction of being among our finest painters. They have something else in common too. All were more or less self-taught and extremely late in reaching painting maturity: three of them were in their late thirties and the fourth, J.E.H. MacDonald, was even older. Is there something about Canada, its geography and climate perhaps, that causes talent to bloom so late?

On his six-month trip to Lakes Huron and Superior in 1845, Kane filled the remaining blank pages of a sketch book he had started in Europe with a series of brilliant watercolours and pencil studies of Ojibway Indian subjects, including portraits of chiefs and squaws and encampment scenes. These colourful works are in striking contrast to the rather hackneyed Venetian and Florentine subjects of this sketch pad.

While on this trip, Kane confided to John Ballenden (spelled Ballantyne by Kane), the Hudson's Bay Company factor at Sault Ste. Marie, his burning ambition to make a trip throughout the far West. Ballenden knew the interior well and cautioned the enthusiastic Kane to consider carefully the perils of attempting such a journey on his own. He advised Kane to seek the support of Governor George Simpson and wrote a letter of recommendation to Simpson praising the artist's sketches and his physical stamina.

George Simpson was an intelligent, tough, and canny Scotsman, whose ambition and propensity for hard work enabled him to climb to the top of the company's ladder, finally becoming Governor-in-Chief of Rupert's Land. A man of complex personality, he had a feeling for history and was deeply interested in the customs and arts of the aborigines. Simpson was now chief of an enterprise that held a virtual monopoly of trading privileges in British North America extending from the St. Lawrence River Basin to the Pacific of which Simpson was to serve as overseas governor for more than thirty years. He was both admired and feared by his colleagues. His power was supreme and he possessed a knowledge of the fur-trading business that was considered legendary.

In March of 1846 Kane went to Lachine where he met Governor Simpson. He showed him sketches and described the trip he wanted to make. Simpson was impressed and undertook to help him.

Kane, with no private means at all, was of course overjoyed at Simpson's decision to allow him the use of the Hudson's Bay Company's travel and lodging facilities and to be permitted to accompany the late spring canoe brigade. Here at last was a golden opportunity to traverse the great Northwestern trading route, if not in absolute comfort at least in the relative security of the experienced Indian guides and voyageurs. Kane had high hopes for action and excitement during the journey and was not to be disappointed.

Kane left Toronto on May 9, 1846, for Sault Ste. Marie, accompanying Simpson on the first leg of one of the governor's trips to the Red River and York Factory; the artist did not return home until October 1848. It was a gruelling journey fraught with danger and full of adventure. In addition, it was the most productive voyage of discovery ever made by a Canadian artist. But what was even more important for posterity was the staggering wealth of primary material he produced. These were pencil, watercolour, and oil-on-paper sketches that would keep him occupied painting them up into medium- and large-sized canvases for the rest of what turned out to be a rather short painting life.

The artist was able to sketch on the spot some of the last great Indian buffalo hunts in 1846. These creatures were being slaughtered by the tens of thousands, even shot from the comfort of railway parlour cars, until, by 1900, they were all but extinct. Thanks to Paul Kane's paintings of these animals the buffalo became almost archetypal to the Canadian eye.

The prairies also afforded him opportunities of painting large Sioux and Métis encampments. On crossing the Rockies he descended the Columbia River to Fort Vancouver (now the State of Washington) in the Oregon Territory, where he spent several weeks studying the life of the Chinook and other neighbouring Indians, making portraits of their principal chiefs and sketching their handsome artifacts. As a further adventure, he set out by canoe with a couple of Indians travelling north across the Strait of Juan de Fuca to Fort Victoria on Vancouver Island.

Simpson had given orders to his factors at various posts along the way to extend special courtesies to the artist and provide him with the necessities of life, as well as transportation, and Kane writes of the kind hospitality extended to him by the factors

14

3   Paul Kane   *The Buffalo Pound*   c.1846

throughout the trip. These favours were of course bestowed at the company's expense and the personal cost to Kane during his two and a half year painting odyssey amounted to practically nothing. This decision on the part of Governor Simpson to sponsor and help Kane must surely be the earliest example of corporate generosity and good will ever extended to a Canadian artist.

Anyone who has read Paul Kane's journal, "Wanderings of an Artist Among the Indians of North America," cannot help but be struck by the staunchness and fortitude of this amazing artist-explorer. By then in his mid-thirties, he was at his physical and artistic prime. Although hard pressed at times by the harsh elements, Kane undertook with relative ease the rigours of travelling through Rocky Mountain passes on horseback, snowshoes and canoe, sometimes in company with Indian guides and sometimes by canoe with the indefatigable voyageurs. Kane was 5'11" tall, the length of his snowshoes. He had a fiery red beard, which, after two years in the wilderness, stretched halfway down his heavy cotton shirts; sometimes it froze and became caked with ice when the temperature fell to forty or more degrees below zero on the trail. Because of his talent in drawing striking likenesses, many Indian chiefs were sure he possessed the powers of a medicine man. Some considered him an alien spirit but others thought of his magic as benign. He also had an eye for a pretty face and painted some of the beautiful young Métis women in their coquettish finery.

While travelling Kane took great care of his precious sketches, some five hundred he claims to have accumulated by the end of his historic journey. His method of packing for transport was simple. Each was put in a portfolio and then several were bundled together and sealed up in oilskins. But there was always the danger of losing baggage when a canoe was hurtling down rapids or of slipping on a rock while fording a swollen stream. Sometimes the packages were carried high on the shoulders of the men crossing rivers on horseback. However, Kane's good luck prevailed to the end. There is no record that he lost a single sketch although some that he had earmarked for Simpson had been slightly "injured" and needed repairs, he noted in his journal.

In Toronto, George William Allan, a lawyer-politician, saw Kane's 1848 City Hall exhibition. He recognized Kane's potential and be-

4   Paul Kane   *A Métis Encampment*   c.1846

came his biggest patron, commissioning one hundred canvases to be worked up from the sketches he had seen. Kane realized how advantageous it would be for him to receive some public patronage as it would automatically give him important recognition. (Cornelius Krieghoff, on the other hand, had many private buyers of his canvases, and never sought or had any support from public funds or government subsidies.)

In July 1850, Kane petitioned the Government of Canada West by letter asking for financial aid to enable him to publish his diaries in book form and produce in commercial quantities lithographs of some of his paintings. No response was forthcoming. A year later the petition was revived and members of a special House Committee visited the artist and were duly impressed with the fascinating Indian material and the quality of the canvases he was then in the process of painting up. In the following year, the legislature voted Kane the sum of £500, commissioning from his brush twelve canvases.

It was not until the 1870s that another well-known personage began to buy Canadian art, namely the irascible journalist-politician and fellow Scot, George Brown, who was busy purchasing works by William Armstrong, John A. Fraser, Lucius O'Brien, Frederick A. Verner, and Henri Perré. We acquired the Brown collection in England in the mid-1950s from George Brown's direct descendants and had the paintings shipped to Canada. At the time, we thought this was quite an historic coup, but it was a minor one compared to our purchase of a significant number of Governor Simpson's sublime paintings by Paul Kane.

By far the artist's staunchest friend was his first patron, the redoubtable Hudson's Bay Governor Sir George Simpson, who was this country's earliest collector of Canadian art. But it was not a friendship Kane always reciprocated.

As early as 1847, while Kane was still in the far West, Simpson wrote him from Lachine that he would like to acquire a dozen sketches of buffalo hunts, council feasts, warlike exhibitions, and any other scenes of "savage life" that "you may consider attractive and interesting." Finally, in January 1849, after nearly two years, Kane sent along ten finished paintings, much finer and more important than ordinary sketches, and promised that another four would follow later.

Freely extending the Hudson's Bay Company's resources, and purchasing pictures, were not the only ways in which Simpson gave a warm and helping hand to Paul Kane. He later gave Kane highly complimentary letters of introduction to his company directors in London, as well as practical advice about the publishing of the Kane journals in book form. Kane, apparently, never sent the additional four pictures on to Simpson, and despite all of Simpson's past assistance, Kane dedicated his book to his later patron, George Allan.

In April 1849, after belatedly informing Simpson of his plans, Kane started out on another western trip that was supposed to last for two years. Kane had hired himself out at a flat fee of £200 per annum, plus expenses. He was expected to act as a guide and interpreter to Sir Edward Poore, a young English army aristocrat, and two of his la-di-da friends. This was such an ill-conceived and foolish venture it is difficult to comprehend Paul Kane's motives for even dreaming to undertake it. Maybe he needed the money. Perhaps he was flattered by Poore's previous purchase of some of his western paintings and could not refuse the offer. But the decision to go on the trip seems especially strange in view of Kane's commitment to complete canvases and fulfil serious commission obligations from his earlier trips.

As it turned out, however, there were strong personality clashes and Poore eventually turned on Kane, castigating him as incompetent and an imposter, claiming he had no knowledge of any Indian tongue. At Fort Garry he fired Kane and paid him off in a fit of rage. The artist then returned home to Toronto with nothing to show for his abbreviated trip except acute embarrassment and unused sketch books.

As far as Simpson was concerned forgotten promises and real or imagined slights finally severed their relationship.

In the preface to the 1925 edition of *Wanderings of an Artist*, Lawrence J. Burpee reminds us that the Simpson paintings "seem to have dropped out of sight." Simpson was so interested in Plains and West Coast Indian subjects that he had intended to design a room for the display of the pictures and artifacts. This project was never realized and time ran out on the governor; he died at Lachine in 1860. His beloved wife, Frances Ramsay Simpson, had predeceased him in 1853.

An incredible interval of 130 years elapsed from the delivery of ten paintings to Simpson at the Bay's headquarters in Lachine in January 1849 to the discovery in 1979 of six Kane paintings in the home of a Simpson descendant in Scotland. It was autumn of the same year while in London that I first got wind that a group of Paul Kane paintings had recently been found in Scotland. Our information was that they might shortly be coming up for sale on the art market by private treaty.

There was nothing much we could do to facilitate action except to await anxiously further contact with the Scottish agent who was our sole link with the pictures' owners. However, this agent-dealer badly needed a valuation for his clients in order to set up a fair selling price. He therefore approached several art auction houses in London, showing the paintings to the appropriate departmental "experts" in an attempt to determine their current market values. This presented a difficult problem as these pictures were treasures of the utmost rarity and to my knowledge nothing like them had ever before appeared on the London auction market that could be used as a precedent. Therefore the young experts' estimates of their value could be made at best by guesswork.

At this stage in the drama I felt something like a player in a game of chance, one unlucky move and the pictures would be gone forever. For instance there was the possibility that the auction houses might present artificially high estimates that would seriously undermine our chances of effectively competing. Then there was always the chance that a national, provincial gallery or archives in Canada might hear of their existence and buy them at high prices with public funds set aside for the return of important Canadian works of art discovered abroad. Up until now the family had considered the pictures of little or no value. But for a twist of fate and Dame Fortune looking benevolently over our shoulders, the Paul Kanes could easily have eluded us. However, situations as delicate as these are not uncommon in the fortunes of war involving dealers who are attempting to buy great pictures in a highly competitive market.

For a while we were left dangling in mid-air, but after what seemed an excruciatingly long wait (actually it was only a fortnight), I at last got to see the pictures. They were works of outstanding quality, all carefully finished oil paintings on paper, some water-

5 Paul Kane *Métis Running Buffalo* c.1846

marked Morbey and Saunders, 1843. These pictures, of uniform size and suitable for framing, had remained safe and sound in an old portfolio in a perfect state of preservation for one and a third centuries. (We still retain the old portfolio in which remain three sheets of the original paper cut to the exact size of the sketches, 9" x 13⅝". These leaves are as strong and fresh as when they were originally made.)

The portfolio contained six sensational oil paintings. One depicted the ancient method of buffalo hunting with Indians and Métis in the act of rounding up a large herd of charging animals while funnelling them through an opening into a fenced-in rough corral, or pound. There is the figure of a medicine man perched high on a tree near the entrance, vigorously waving brightly coloured pieces of cloth, beseeching the Great Spirit to send the buffalo through the narrow opening into the stockade; his magic was simple and effective. These paintings could also be considered as primitive; all the buffalo, for example, are running or standing in the same position. These events, of course, took place before the general use of the camera, so the exact position of the legs of animals while in full flight remained a mystery. Kane's buffalo pictures are somewhat reminiscent of prehistoric paintings of the bison in Spain's Altamira cave.

Another in the portfolio was a serene view of a group of buffalo resting or grazing in a peaceful valley. It was a day in Indian Summer in 1846 not far from Fort Carlton, and Kane extols the beauty of the scenery which lies along the banks of the Saskatchewan River. The vast prairies seem to have ended in that serene rolling meadow by the river, where the pasture was sweet and verdant and the forms of the animals, especially their great bearded heads, loomed out monumentally like their prehistoric cousins.

Two more depicted groups of naked Indians netting and spearing salmon during a run on the Columbia River, some standing on rough wooden piers, some poised on the edge of high banks awaiting the proper moment to hurl their long wooden spears. These paintings were fresh and colourful, reflecting an immediacy and liveliness of the subjects, suffused as they were in either the clear, bright light of high noon prairie skies, or, as in the case of the Indians salmon fishing, the wetter maritime atmosphere of the Pacific Coast.

22

The fifth was another painting of a Sioux-Métis encampment with scores of buffalo-skin teepees deftly pitched on the flat terrain and arranged by Kane in eye-pleasing geometric pattern with horses grazing nearby. The sixth depicted a group of thirty or more mounted Métis, galloping at full speed in wedge form into the heart of a buffalo herd. It graphically suggests a cavalry charge, or an English fox hunt, except, in this case, the quarries are the unwitting buffalo.

Because of size and paper format, it is now my positive belief that the two oil paintings on paper, *Drying Salmon on the Dalles, Columbia River* and *Clallum Indian Travelling Lodges, Vancouver Island* (perhaps not Kane's original titles) which I found in London some twenty years earlier, and which were reproduced in my first book, were also two of Simpson's commissioned works, but from another branch of the family.

By my reckoning, then, this would leave only two of Sir George's ten Kane paintings unaccounted for.

In the spring of 1980, a well-dressed couple walked into our gallery specifically looking for nineteenth-century Canadian works. In a chance remark the young woman spoke of a recent discovery of some rare Paul Kane paintings. She was referring, of course, to the six Paul Kane paintings that had recently come into our possession in London. She was an art historian who by hard work and a long period of research, including a trip to Scotland, had succeeded in tracking down, through descendants of Sir George Simpson, some of the Paul Kane paintings that Simpson had commissioned from Kane in 1847. Apparently nobody previously had thought of the logic of tracing the sketches by checking with any living Simpson descendant in Scotland. Her name is Susan J. Stewart and she has published an excellent article on the six pictures we have been referring to in *The Journal of Canadian Art History*, vol. V, no. 2, 1981, pp. 85-93.

Concurrent with her discovery, others in Scotland learned about the cache, having no doubt been informed by members of the Simpson family. For us it was a touchy situation and a lot depended on just how much was known by the relatives and their advisors about the importance of both Sir George Simpson's place in Canadian history and the even greater niche that Paul Kane had carved for himself as one of the fathers of Canadian art. Had this information caught the attention of Canadian art circles it would have made an exciting story for the press and the owners or their agents no doubt would have been bombarded with offers from Canada to buy. I was staying at my favourite hotel in London, the Savoy, when I finally received a call from my partner, his voice husky with excitement. In great elation he cried, "Blair, we've got the pictures!" The winning ticket was simply our ability to complete the transaction immediately and for cash.

There was yet another artist of consequence who had a connection with the Hudson's Bay Company, and whose elegant canvases and attractive watercolours we have had from time to time. Her name was Frances Ann Hopkins. Kane noted in his journal that on the 27th of May 1846, Sir George Simpson passed him with his two canoes, accompanied by his secretary, Mr. Hopkins. Martin Hopkins was a good secretary. He and his first wife, Annie Ogden Hopkins, were a favourite couple of Sir George and Lady Frances and were often Sunday dinner guests at Lachine. Annie died of cholera in 1854 and four years later, E.M. Hopkins was remarried to Frances Anne Beechey, the twenty-year-old daughter of the late Rear Admiral Frederick William Beechey of Arctic fame. Frances, who came to live at Lachine, was a talented artist and while accompanying her husband on various trips to the Red River sketched and painted subjects of the upper Great Lakes including camp sites and studies of the great freight canoes which their voyageur paddlers could move through the water with effortless rhythm and remarkable speed.

In September 1951, my colleague and London partner, Tom Baskett, and I decided to visit Paul Kane III at his home in Winnipeg. It was the right thing to do, but definitely the wrong moment to talk to Mr. Kane, and nothing came of the meeting.

He lived in a small, white, frame house south of the Assiniboine River and was one of those old-time Manitoba lawyers, retired from practice. We found him a disgruntled and dispirited man and he seemed tired and ill. He informed us, not without a sense of bitterness, that his long-lasting attempts to sell his Kane collection to the Government of Canada, through the offices of Prime Minister Mackenzie King, had met with no success. The asking price was $100,000, but unfortunately Mr. King had never shown any interest

6   Frances A. Hopkins   *Voyageurs and Mrs. Hopkins on the Upper Great Lakes*   c.1870

in Canadian art.

As I recall the scene now, Paul Kane III, Tom Baskett and I sat around his dining-room table examining some of the pencil sketches he had brought out. The old man had a strong intuitive feeling that his grandfather's sketches represented a highly important segment of early Canadian art; but in general, the small group of pencil studies he showed us were minor drawings and nothing to get excited about. Although he did say there were others, Mr. Kane did not give us the slightest hint of their significance and that he was sitting on what was the final great cache of Paul Kane pictures in Canada. Had we known of the existence of these superior and colourful works he had stored away, I am sure we would have made a great effort to convince him to at least show them to us.

In 1955-56 Paul Kane III offered his collection to Eric Harvie, one of the early Calgary oil millionaires, who had recently founded the Glenbow Foundation. Mr. Harvie, probably making his decision without sufficient investigation, found the price excessive and passed up what turned out to be the final opportunity to keep the Kane collection in Canada.

In 1957, a shocked outcry greeted the news that T.H.J. Lutcher Stark of Texas had bought some 230 watercolours, oils, and pencil sketches by the hand of Paul Kane, from the Kane family for $100,000. Alan Jarvis was then director of the National Gallery, and was quoted in the press as saying: "We turned down the purchase because we did not want the whole block." As if by a stroke of fate, Paul Kane III died within one year of the sale.

The Starks recognized Kane as the portrayer of North American Indian life unsurpassed by any other artist of his time, and a gallery was built in Orange, Texas and not in Winnipeg, Manitoba, where it should have been to show the work of Paul Kane III's illustrious grandfather. It was not until J. Russell Harper's book, *Paul Kane's Frontier*, was published in 1971, that I fully realized how immensely important was the Kane collection still in family hands in the 1950s. Harper's book reproduced dozens of superb watercolours which, of course, I never saw in Mr. Kane's house on that September day in 1951.

This little group of Governor Simpson's Paul Kane paintings, totally unique in format and finish, is now more important than ever, especially since the Kane family collection crossed our borders for Texas.

26

7   Paul Kane   *Salmon Fishing, Columbia River*   c.1846

8 Cornelius Krieghoff *Habitants Going to Market* 1848

2

Cornelius Krieghoff — Some Friends and Early Patrons

Cornelius Krieghoff was just five years younger than Paul Kane. These two men may have met each other during Krieghoff's brief visit to Toronto in 1845, but considering the difference in their painting visions and ethnic and cultural backgrounds even a casual friendship could hardly have been possible. Also, Kane himself, during this final decade of his life, became more and more retiring and taciturn as he gradually lost his sight.

Cornelius Krieghoff, on the other hand, was much more outgoing, an artist and musician with Romany gypsy-like characteristics who entered enthusiastically into the fun and high-jinks of habitant life. Krieghoff's Indian studies depicted them in peaceful pursuits, camping on lake shores or snowshoeing with toboggans in tow. By the mid-1840s, the Indians of Lorette and Caugnawaga, were content to live on reserves alongside white settlements and participate in occasional hunting parties. As a people they were vastly different to the more primitive and sometimes war-like tribes of the Plains and West Coast. Krieghoff himself made few sallies into the hinterland, finding satisfaction in painting the more domesticated scenes around Montreal and Quebec. Thus Kane and Krieghoff each had their own unique painting visions.

Born in Holland, in 1815, of a German father and a mother who was probably a Netherlander, much of Cornelius Krieghoff's early life remains a mystery. Born with a natural ear for music he also had a precocious eye and taste for art. In his youth he toured Europe as an itinerant musician and took every opportunity to copy and study the technique of the Old Masters. A tireless worker, I estimate he produced up to 2,000 works, both large and small, during a painting career that spanned about two and a half decades in Canada, and he sold more pictures by far than all the other artists of his period put together. Except for short teaching stints in colleges for young ladies in Montreal and Quebec City, he devoted his full time to painting, and during the final twenty years or so of his life was able to live nicely from the labours of his brush.

Krieghoff's small self-portrait of 1855 is a remarkable example of an artist's search into his inner self. It reveals a dark-haired, full-bearded man of forty years with deep-set, serious eyes. His swarthy countenance makes one wonder if his forbears might indeed have been Romany gypsies who roamed through central Europe in their caravans, dancing and merrymaking. Maybe there was some gypsy blood in Krieghoff and that's why he responded so positively to the character of the French Canadian habitants and captured their spirit of living so well.

What other painter of his time could have done this and produced such visual masterpieces as *The Morning After Merrymaking* or *Playtime Village School*? For some time he lived with his French-Canadian wife at Longueuil in her family home, and, speaking their language, got to know the habitant people intimately. He was also quick to learn and to understand their foibles and ways.

With his brush he soon became a skilled and dedicated artist who interpreted and captured the vitality of French Canada. Krieghoff's point of view was definitely humanistic. This was quite different from the topographers of the period who were primarily concerned with the landscape that engulfed them. Marius Barbeau, the eminent folklorist, speculates that Krieghoff was of Polish-Jewish extraction, but he could also have been of Russian stock. Whatever that background was, it contributed to his ability to interpret the life and times of mid-nineteenth-century Quebec. He produced compositions of great *élan* and quixotic humour. This is the legacy the artist has left and Canadian culture would be much the poorer without it.

By the early 1860s, however, though still only in his late forties, he seems suddenly to have grown old. No one really knows what it was that made him appear at least fifteen years older than he actually was. During this period his painting production began to fall off drastically. It is hard to believe that it was the same person who painted the humorous and saucy incidents of French-Canadian village life with such verve and affection just a few years earlier.

Around 1847 Krieghoff, probably in Montreal, met a young Englishman, whose association and comradeship would exert quite an influence during some of the artist's most productive years. His name was John S. Budden. In the same year Krieghoff painted an informal portrait of his elegant new friend sitting under a tree with his dog and a sporting rifle lying nearby on the ground, a tall silk hat beside it.

Budden, a transplanted Londoner, was probably a remittance man, and able to live quite comfortably on an assured income from family sources in England. Well cultivated, and a person of charm and wit, he enjoyed his role as Quebec City's mid-nineteenth-century version of "a man about town." He also boasted a summer home in nearby Montmorency. It is not known whether he was just an employee or a partner in A.J. Maxim's local auction house which sold antiques, household goods, and cheap chromos imported from England, but Budden preferred the excitement of the winter sports, moose hunting, or fishing the Atlantic salmon to the humdrum life of the ordinary business world. Budden, a bachelor, also enjoyed art and was fascinated with Kreighoff's canvases; he also admired the artist's linguistic and musical talents.

It is worth while noting that these two men of totally different backgrounds formed a relationship that turned into what was probably the first artist-dealer partnership in Canada. As early as 1851, Budden actually procured pictures from Kreighoff on consignment to place in auction sales in Quebec City while the artist was still in Montreal with a studio on St. James Street. Then, about a year later, Budden, who remained in constant touch with the artist, finally persuaded him to move to Quebec City and set up a studio there. Budden convinced Krieghoff that sales would be better in

Quebec and his judgement turned out to be correct, as during the next nine or ten years, Krieghoff, having happily settled down in Quebec City, produced a large number of his finest works. Unlike many artists whose colour sense deteriorated as they grew older, Krieghoff's remained vibrant until the end of his life.

According to Marius Barbeau's delightful and romantic account of the life and times of Cornelius Krieghoff, the figure of John Budden became more and more involved with the artist and his work. Budden introduced him to prospective customers, sold his pictures, and generally acted as his agent. Working with an artist of Cornelius Krieghoff's stature was a challenge to the enthusiastic Budden and likewise Budden's services were appreciated by the hard-working painter, and they long remained good friends.

Among the people whom John Budden introduced to Krieghoff was James Gibb, the wealthy Quebec City lumber dealer. The artist in an important canvas had immortalized the pug-nosed, genial Mr. Gibb by painting a full-length image of him on snow-shoes, flanked by full-length portraits of both the artist and John Budden, standing in the snow beside a fallen moose. The magnificence of their hunting dress rivals the awesome beauty of the landscape. James Gibb was to become Krieghoff's most important patron. He bought either direct from the artist himself, or, in the case of a large *Merrymaking* canvas, from one of Kreighoff's personally sponsored auction sales of 1862, when over 100 of his pictures were sold in Quebec under the hammer. On Mr. Gibb's death the collection was left to his widow who later married a John Ross. Some of the pictures have remained in the Ross family to this day, so that more than 120 years have elapsed since their original acquisition from the artist.

Another contemporary collector-patron was Alexander Ross, no relation to the above-mentioned John. He was engineer-in-chief of the Grand Trunk Railway and designer of Montreal's Victoria Bridge. A niece wrote a letter to Marius Barbeau in the early 1930s explaining that her uncle had at one time more than forty Kreighoff pictures. Curiously, when her uncle died, the paintings were hanging in the office of his brother, Hugh Ross, in London. Five were later bequeathed to her cousin, Clementine, then living in Montreal, some were sold in England, and the rest were divided

9 Cornelius Krieghoff *In the Jardin des Cariboux, Fifty Miles Below Quebec* c.1860

among relatives living in England, Australia, and New Zealand. This was a collection larger in number than Gibb's but the individual pictures were not as important as those that Mr. Gibb had selected for himself.

Then there was the Alexander Simpson collection. Simpson, who had been the chief cashier of the Bank of Montreal, retired in 1855 to return to Scotland. These pictures remained in a Scottish family until more than 100 years later when they were auctioned off in London. One of them, which I bought at the sale, was a winter scene with horse-drawn sleigh and figures in a snow-covered valley with the Laurentians providing a spectacular backdrop. It was circular in shape and one of the very few examples of the artist's work that remained in the original frame that Krieghoff had made to order by his Philadelphia frame makers, James S. Earle and Son.

Besides making frames for Krieghoff it is almost certain that the Earle firm handled and sold his paintings, too, as over the years several large canvases have turned up in the Philadelphia area. Beside the Youngs, Sir Alexander Galt, and other Scottish-born Quebec residents, Canada's Governor General the Earl of Elgin, was also a patron. A century later we were to buy Krieghoff pictures from the present Elgin, his descendant.

By far his most consistent buyers were the British army officers, stationed at the great Citadel (most of whose names are now lost within the dim corridors of history). They brought or sent his pictures home to Britain as special gifts and prized souvenirs. Many of the paintings once owned by these colourful pioneer art collectors, including the officer buyers, have over a period of forty years or more come into our possession through family descendants, and those discovered in Britain have nearly all been returned by us to Canada.

The nineteenth-century Montreal picture dealer and frame maker, William Scott, knew the artist and during Krieghoff's lifetime probably showed some of his pictures in his Montreal shop. After the artist's death in 1872 Scott and Sons continued buying and selling Krieghoff paintings until the firm closed its doors for good in 1939.

The other Montreal dealer who specialized in handling the works of Krieghoff was William R. Watson. Watson, my father's contemporary, possessed a strange bird-like face. His lower lip had a prominent blue-black spot of pigmentation, which, however, lent a positive character to his countenance. Watson often placed in his street window paintings which had on them a red star, or sometimes half a red star. The former denoted that the picture was already sold and the latter that the picture was on reserve for a special customer. This often annoyed prospective buyers but the criticism didn't bother Mr. Watson at all. In fact he considered this routine as a bit of a tease, as he liked to show off to the passing public on Sherbrooke Street some of his best pictures even though they weren't for sale. He also fancied himself as a picture restorer. On occasion I saw him in the process of cleaning a Kreighoff painting using a solvent to remove the discoloured varnish and then mounting the canvas on a piece of masonite which, strictly speaking, was not a professional thing to do. However, permanent damage seldom resulted and it was not difficult to remove the canvas from this support and then reline it in conventional fashion.

Watson was an enthusiastic admirer of the paintings of Krieghoff and whenever I visited his gallery in Montreal, which was usually four or five times a year, there would always be a canvas or two by this artist on hand. He once confided that his greatest ambition was to have an exhibition and sale of the works of Krieghoff, but this never became possible because he couldn't stockpile enough paintings for such an event. He used to regale me with amusing stories, one since repeated in his autobiography was about how he once discovered two bundles of pictures by Cornelius Krieghoff tied together with string in the rooms of a small auction house in London. Rather than risk a bidding competition and thereby push up the price, he was able to buy them for nothing by having a London cabby bid for him by pre-arranged signals.

William Watson also collaborated with Marius Barbeau in producing the splendid, but by today's standards incomplete, *catalogue raisonné* of the works of Cornelius Krieghoff as an adjunct to Barbeau's book, *Cornelius Krieghoff, Pioneer Painter in North America*, published in 1934. We had a good relationship with William R. Watson and bought many pictures from him. When he decided to retire from business in 1958 he gave us first chance to buy all or any part of his entire stock. My father and I travelled together to Montreal and made a deal that allowed us to acquire a large part of it, including some thirty watercolour paintings by Frederick A.

Verner, another nineteenth-century Canadian artist whose work Watson firmly believed in.

Watson also specialized in the work of Maurice Cullen, the great Newfoundland-born, Quebec-based, Post-Impressionist landscape painter. However, like other art dealers in Montreal, he was forced to show and sell the work of popular European artists because of the lack of interest in Canadian art. Watson deserves more than passing credit in becoming one of Montreal's best and most reliable dealers. When you see a Watson label on a picture he has previously sold, you can be absolutely sure it is a genuine work by the artist represented.

There were extremely few Krieghoff collectors after the artist's death in 1872, and general commerce in art was dormant for nearly the next fifty years. Indeed, art dealers were almost nonexistent during the last century and it was not until a few years before the Great War that much original art was sold in Canada. Such industrial titans as Sir William Van Horne bought all their pictures in Europe and New York. Therefore Krieghoff's pictures remained more or less with the original families for a half a century or more. Some perished in Quebec fires, like the one at John Budden's; other works have simply disappeared.

It was during the 1920s that a small group of Krieghoff collectors appeared on the buying horizon. A notable pair were Harry Norton and his sister Helen, who inherited substantial wealth from their father, a successful inventor. By 1934, they together owned at least seventeen good canvases. Also Ward C. Pitfield, the brilliant Montreal financier, acquired some master works by Krieghoff through the Philadelphia Slater family originally sold by the Earle Gallery. Then there was Robert W. Reford, the Montreal shipping magnate, and William H. Coverdale, president of the Canada Steamship Lines, who were both avid collectors of Canadiana during the late twenties and thirties when few people were at all interested. Gordon C. Edwards inherited some fine examples from his uncle William C., the lumber dealer senator from Ottawa, including *Habitant's Home in Winter*, which we bought from Mr. Edwards in 1949, and sold a little later to Harold Connell of Connell brothers mining fame. Earlier we had acquired the subject *Bargaining Wood* from the A.E. Beck family in Toronto. We first sold this canvas in 1942, to a Mr. Jones and later bought it back

10   Cornelius Krieghoff   *Bargaining Wood*   c.1855

from the owner when he got into a terrible tax jam, and desperately needed money to pay a fine, the government having nailed him for wartime profiteering.

One of our most unlikely patrons during the forties was Robert Elliot, a rugged Canadian Scot who made a business of making deals with prospectors on mining claims. For some years he operated a general store in the Noranda district of northwestern Quebec, and a sideline to his business was grubstaking prospectors with food and other supplies. They, in turn, were expected to repay him with a percentage in any claims they staked. Sometimes he received shares in a new company about to be listed on the stock exchange before the stock was actually offered to the public. Although hard as nails in business, this man had his genial side as well with a certain old-fashioned integrity that was most refreshing. He possessed a keen if untutored interest in art, and began to assemble, with my father's help and advice, a good Canadian collection with emphasis on the nineteenth-century artists. He eventually acquired a dozen or more fine canvases by Cornelius Krieghoff, including such important works as *Bargaining Wood*, mentioned earlier, and a fine version of the *Running the Toll Gate* series.

In those days Bob Elliot owned a spunky charcoal-coloured Kerry blue terrier called Clancy, who regularly accompanied his master on downtown visits to the luxurious offices of his mining company clients where a lesser dog-character than Clancy would have been unceremoniously thrown out. It was during appointments with those people that he worked out his complicated stock option deals. Robert Elliot possessed a special knack for figures which was quite remarkable at a time when pocket computers weren't yet invented. He was a friend of my father's whose advice on the buying of pictures he followed implicitly.

In the mid-fifties, after a break-in burglary at his house, Bob Elliott reluctantly decided to sell his splendid group of Krieghoffs to the controversial mining promotor M.J. Boylen after first consulting my father regarding a proper price. Like other mining entrepreneurs that I knew, Boylen was a powerfully built man of medium height easily able to cope with the rigours of the bush in all seasons. Extremely tough by nature and mentally sharp, he was an individualist, full of energy and boundless ambition. He started his working life as a trapper and a fur trader at the age of fourteen and, at seventeen, became a full-time mining prospector, who put together a group of mining claims near Larder Lake in Northern Ontario. His greatest piece of good luck was the discovery of the rich Bathurst mining territory in New Brunswick, which really set him up for life, as he had sworn that nothing would ever stand in his way of one day becoming rich and famous.

In the early fifties Boylen began to buy decorative European pictures for a large house he had purchased in the Toronto Kingsway district, and shortly afterwards became interested in the paintings of Cornelius Krieghoff. We sold him several, including for $15,000 a large winter landscape with many wondrously placed figures entitled *Return From the Village*. I remember at the time he argued fiercely that the price was too high and that we were ahead of the market, but the picture was of such superior quality and the subject matter of such great interest that he just couldn't bear to pass it by. Boylen often called me for information and advice when, among other things, he needed current insurance valuations. At one time, I remember twenty-seven splendid canvases by Krieghoff hanging on the walls of the sitting room in his Kingsway home.

About 1956, Jim Boylen was introduced to the famous but sometimes mischievous Lord Beaverbrook, to whom he later presented some of his Krieghoff paintings (though not the best ones) to be hung in the splendid new public art gallery in Fredericton that Beaverbrook was building as a gift to the province. His lordship, being chancellor of the University of New Brunswick, returned the favour at a convocation by bestowing on Mr. Boylen the title of doctor of laws. Jim Boylen was extremely proud of both his honorary degree and his Krieghoff paintings.

Unlike Robert Elliot, who never became wealthy or well-known at all, Boylen successfully achieved some of the prime goals of his life, prestige and wealth. But, unfortunately, he died too soon to come to terms with humility and realize any equanimity of spirit. He spent the final part of his life in clinics in the United States, vainly trying to regain some of his former robust health.

A man who had become wealthy for inventing and selling successfully a new type of washing machine, W.M. Connor of Ottawa, became fascinated with Krieghoff and began to buy his paintings during the 1930s, continuing to acquire them until the mid-1940s, when after his only son was killed in the war he abruptly lost interest in further collecting.

During the late 1940s, and into the early fifties, Connor began to sell us some of his Krieghoffs and once, while visiting his Ottawa home, among the works of other Canadian artists, I counted no less than thirty Krieghoffs hanging on the walls. He had bought most of them from William R. Watson and the Scott and Sons firm in Montreal. Later he had a vision of turning over his whole collection to the National Gallery of Canada as a memorial to his son provided that institution would permanently house it. This ambition was thwarted as the gallery officials and the trustees were then unable or unwilling to grant his request. Furthermore in those days most gallery curators showed little interest in Krieghoff's work. Today, of course, some way would have been found to take advantage of such a generous proposal. Finally Mr. Connor made up his mind that he would, with minor exceptions, turn over his entire collection for sale by an auction house in London.

Although it was never our business policy to store pictures for customers, from time to time for various reasons we did so. Sometimes people brought in pictures for examination and then left them with us for periods varying from a few weeks to twenty-five years or more, as was the case with Winnifred Trainor's Tom Thomson sketches. At some point if not the owners themselves, then their heirs, would eventually arrive to collect the stored works.

Recently, there was the curious case of someone leaving a valuable painting with us and then disappearing. He happened to be the great-grandson of Ernest Krieghoff, Cornelius Krieghoff's brother, both of whom had sailed to New York in the late 1830s. The following incident describes what took place in the spring of 1972, during my absence from Toronto. The beginning of this strange story was related to me by my mother who usually remained in charge of the business when I was away on buying or selling trips.

It was in mid-May of that year, as my mother tells the story, that a sallow-faced man came into the gallery with a framed picture under his arm. Looking spent and ill, he immediately sat down on the nearest gallery bench to rest. "My name is Krieghoff," he announced listlessly as he unwrapped a smallish canvas in a battered old frame. "This picture is by my great-uncle Cornelius and I would like to have it restored." My mother explained that I was away until the following week, and that it would be necessary for me to look at it personally to see if we could handle the work. The gentleman said that he would return next week and asked if we would hold the picture for him. He then walked out the front door and disappeared. It was to be eight full years before we heard from him again.

In his abrupt departure, he had left no mailing address, and there was no identification or ownership clue on the parcel. I had no intention of proceeding with any restoration work until I could talk to the owner and give him a proper estimate. Consequently we put the package away on our basement shelves along with other unclaimed pictures, and it was soon forgotten.

Then one day, eight years later, we received a letter addressed as follows: "Art Gallery, Toronto," and signed by a Ned Krieghoff, enquiring if we still had his Cornelius Krieghoff painting. The delivery to us of a letter with no name or address on the envelope was indeed a brilliant deduction on the part of the post office. The only clue to the sender's whereabouts was an address on Madison Avenue, Detroit. I checked with the telephone directory service and discovered it was the street number of the Detroit Athletic Club. I promptly telephoned the club, and, quite by chance Mr. Krieghoff was put on the line. He apparently lunched at the Athletic Club every day, and also used it as a mailing address. "Your picture is here," I informed him. "It has been stored away and took a while to locate." I could sense, over the telephone wire, his great relief, and he said he would be in touch with me soon.

Several days passed before I received a one-sentence letter in his slanted, shaky hand. "What will the picture realize on the market?" The picture was a typical winter sleigh scene and I wrote giving him an estimate of probable value. Then, in a matter of days, another letter arrived. Its complete text was, "Do you have any news? Best regards, Ned Krieghoff."

We did indeed find a buyer, and Mr. Kreighoff, delighted with the news when I talked with him again, said he would come to Toronto immediately to pick up the money. "I would like it split equally in U.S. and Canadian funds," he advised.

When he finally arrived at our galleries I found that his physical appearance coincided almost perfectly with my mother's description of the man of eight years earlier; he still looked old and worn out. Born in 1914, as we found out later, exactly a century less one year separated his birth and that of Cornelius Krieghoff. Indeed, he retained a close facial resemblance to his ancestor uncle that was quite uncanny, especially the square jaw and high cheekbones. He was polite, amicable, and easy to do business with. He apologized as unforgivable the fact that he had left the picture unclaimed for all those years, and blamed his lapse of memory on serious business problems. I had the strong feeling that one reason he felt so pleased with the sale was that it came as a big relief to find that until that time the painting had neither been sold nor irrevocably misplaced. He realized that if that had been the case, there would have been little to be done about it. I believe, too, that D. Edwin Krieghoff, Jr. really got his money when he needed it most.

Throughout the years there have been some helpful picture dealers in England who have come into possession or otherwise discovered Krieghoff pictures in remote or out of the way places in the British Isles. For example, in 1955, the prominent dealer in Old Masters, David Koetser (now working out of Zurich), discovered a cache of five Krieghoffs in Ireland and turned them over to us to sell. One was a *Clearing of the Land* subject, a fair-sized vertical piece depicting a French-Canadian peasant cutting down a tree. Later we sold this picture to Dr. Morton Shulman, who some years later resold it at a handsome profit.

The expert London picture restorers, Charles and Sidney Hahn, over a period of fifteen years or so found and sold to us at least twenty-five canvases by Kreighoff, and had superbly cleaned and restored each one of them. From 1951 to 1963 we bought these paintings in half-share ownership with the London P. & D. Colnaghi Company through a partner, D.C.T. Baskett, and they all came to Canada.

We made many trips to western Canada and during those years of plentiful supply we always had a selection of Krieghoffs for sale. Following Tom Baskett's death in 1962 the Colnaghi firm lost interest in its Canadian business and we bought them out. We then began to do business with another London-based firm, Williams and Son. Williams had early connections in Canada, especially Toronto, but had also sold paintings by Krieghoff to William Watson in Montreal. Then there was the Toronto branch of the London Cooling firm which dealt in the nineteenth-century landscape and genre pictures. They too bought paintings by Krieghoff in the old country and showed many until they closed their little gallery on the death

11 Cornelius Krieghoff *Indians at the Big Rock, Near Quebec* c.1860

of Herbert Cooling in 1964.

There was another significant place in London where we found paintings by Krieghoff and Paul Kane, a veritable treasure house in the mid-1950s, a sort of wholesale place where hundreds of pictures were piled against the walls and in racks reaching from floor to ceiling. The business was operated by the two Appleby brothers and you never knew when you might discover something superb there. This energetic pair took turns searching all over the country and attending auction sales in out of the way small towns and villages. This wonderful store house had been set in an old building just behind Trafalgar Square. Today, alas, it is nothing more than a memory.

In all the years we sought out his work, I have never seen any black and white pencil or pen and ink drawings by Cornelius Krieghoff. However, we did discover several of his small watercolours in England, and a large one too, on an imperial-sized drawing sheet (22″ x 30″). It was a version of his famous *Bilking the Toll* series, a magnificent work as carefully finished as many of his larger oils. I would dearly love to find one of his sketch books, such as the kind you see the artist holding while portraying himself in one of his memorable landscapes. Whether any of these drawings will ever come to light now is extremely doubtful. I expect any sketch books that remained after the artist's death, were destroyed by fire on the Quebec premises of John Budden back in the 1880s.

Of all the work of Canadian artists of the nineteenth century, Cornelius Krieghoff's paintings were the most consistently admired and widely collected during his lifetime, and now, in the 1980s, they are sought after more than ever before.

3

The Bishop's Journal

In the latter years of the eighteenth century, and through-out nearly three quarters of the century following, there were a number of well-trained officer-artists serving in the British army and navy, career soldiers and sailors. During their basic training years in England many had the good fortune to be tutored by excellent drawing masters in the renowned military and naval academies of their time.

On tours of duty in Canada and also when posted else-where in the empire they made landscape and topographical studies, and regularly kept meticulous diaries and notebook chronicles. They drew over and over such sights as the Quebec Citadel from the St. Lawrence River, Montmorency Falls in summer and in winter topped by its spectacular ice cone, which they considered one of nature's sublime creations. Here the fun-loving habitants and visitors from nearby Quebec enjoyed to the full the zestful winter sports, whizzing down from the summit on sleighs and toboggans. Then some hundreds of miles upstream, between two of the Great Lakes, was the awesome spectacle of Niagara Falls which they nearly all drew or painted at some time or other.

Some of these military and naval people, dedicated to the services, were excellent artists, map-makers, and topographers. They usually came from aristocratic upper-class families and the landed gentry. It was a common practice of the well-to-do to pur-

45

12   Lt. Col. James P. Cockburn   *The Waterfall*   c.1826

13   George Heriot   *View of Halifax from the Harbour*   c.1805

chase army commissions for their sons and many of these young men became capable officers. There were misfits, too, but most of these were quickly discharged from the services – the profession of an officer was universally accepted as a right and honourable status in life. Well educated in the arts of war, some of them also had the opportunity of studying drawing and watercolour painting under the direction of skilled professional artists on the staff of the British military and naval academies.

Some of these army artists discovered parts of Canada's vast landscape sixty or more years before our twentieth century landscape school began. There were even earlier ones too, like Lt. Col. James P. Cockburn, famous for his published series of engravings of Niagara Falls. George Heriot, deputy postmaster general of British North America from 1800-1816, who painted exquisite little watercolours, and Lt. General Davies, who painted extensively in Canada in the final years of the eighteenth century.

Albums of these watercolours and pen and pencil drawings are Canada's cultural heritages of a very high order, and it is gratifying to find that some still surface through descendants of the officers and their families after being hidden away for a century or more in a library or closet. As members of one of Canada's two founding races, English-speaking Canadians are prone to forget the original roles of these ancestral soldiers who contributed art forms that tell us certain things about their life and times that otherwise we would know much less about today. Instead we should cherish these artistic mementoes.

For nearly fifty years, England proved to be a rich reservoir of early Canadian art treasures, providing us with a significant supply of works painted in Canada during the nineteenth century. In 1958, my London partner, D.C.T. Baskett of Colnaghi's, discovered in England through one of his antiquarian bookseller friends, two mid-nineteenth-century albums filled with original drawings and watercolours of Canadian and American topographical interest. Tom Baskett, always on the alert, had a talent for uncovering and acquiring unusual pieces of art. At the time, there was little interest in such items and the total cost for the two albums amounted to less than £100. However, from a Canadiana viewpoint they were unique artists' records, and I was glad to acquire them and put them away for future consideration. These drawings being on separate

14   Francis A. Grant   *Lord Elgin Leaving for Parliament, Montreal*   1849

pages were easily removed from their albums so they could be safely placed on the classic English wash-lined mounts that suited them so well. They were then packaged up into small bundles and the entire collection was shipped to Toronto where they remained stored away on our basement shelves for the next twenty-three years. The two albums accounted for a total of nearly 150 frameable items. During 1980, while working on some nineteenth-century pictorial material for this book, I decided to examine these drawings and watercolours more carefully. I hoped they might reveal some fresh aspects of life in Canada during those times – and I feel they do.

The first album consisted entirely of pen and pencil drawings, and nearly all were signed F.A. Grant. These sketches, of various dimensions, have proved to be of considerable merit and historical value.

The artist was obviously a trained draftsman who occasionally displayed flashes of humour in his work. Initially all I knew about this person was that his name was Grant; but while studying the drawings I noted a *Horse and Sleigh* study, signed and dated Montreal, 1849. What intrigued me was the artist's own inscription, "Sketched from the Aide-De-Camp's waiting room." This was an interesting clue. Could F.A. Grant have been a member of Lord Elgin's staff since this illustrious Englishman was Canada's Governor General at the time?

In the Victorian era the British aristocracy produced an astonishing number of talented administrators and able diplomats, well trained and adaptable. They seemed born and bred for the duties of managing the affairs of Her Majesty's Government, both at home and abroad. James Bruce, 8th Earl of Elgin, Governor General of Canada from 1846 to 1854, was one of them. The Elgin family had long been involved in the arts. It was his father, Thomas Bruce, 7th Earl of Elgin, a connoisseur of classical sculpture who, with the acquiescence of the Turks, arranged for the removal of some of the great marbles from the battered Athens Parthenon to the British Museum in London, where they are now on view. During his term of office as Governor General of Canada, Lord Elgin lived in the governor's mansion in Montreal and was almost certainly a patron of the Quebec artist, Cornelius Krieghoff, and possibly knew Paul Kane as well. We have handled at one time or another at least four of Krieghoff's winter scenes depicting the

Montreal 1849.
Sketched from the A D C's waiting room — F A Grant

15   Francis A. Grant   *A Montreal Horse Cab*   (sketched from the A.D.C.'s waiting room)   1849

governor and his lady driving in an elegant carriole in town, at Montmorency, or on the ice-bound St. Lawrence. These appeared in England over the years and came from descendants of the Elgin family.

My curiosity about Grant's identity was aroused and I began to study the remaining sketches. I soon found a larger and more detailed pen and ink drawing inscribed *Lord Elgin and Staff Leaving Government House for Parliament, Montreal, 1849*. There are four horses drawn up at the mansion entrance with two outriders waiting for the governor to step into his carriage while a group of mounted horse-guards attentively stand by.

I could see from the sketches that Grant was also an accomplished horseman who enjoyed nothing better than participating in hunting and racing meets. He must have accompanied Elgin on nearly all his journeys, recording their travels in his sketch book, including a trip through the Great Lakes by paddle steamer, with a stopover at Manitoulin Island to meet and converse with Indian chiefs. According to Grant's sketches, Lord Elgin visited Chatham and Sault Ste. Marie, and Grant even draws the governor on horseback attending a ploughing match near Toronto. In another pen drawing entitled *A Yankee Stage Coach in the State of Vermont, Summer of 1852*, Grant's use of the derogatory term "Yankee," expresses the social and political bias against the American presence in nearby Vermont, typical of that time.

I discovered that F.A. Grant was a nephew of Lord Elgin, and his full name was Francis Augustus Grant. He had been born into an aristocratic Scottish family at Kilgraston, Perthshire, in 1829. His mother was the daughter of the 7th Earl of Elgin, and therefore James Bruce was the artist's uncle.

In 1847 Grant purchased a commission as an ensign with the Queen's Own Cameron Highlanders (79th Regiment of Foot) and, in 1850, he was promoted to lieutenant. As a young officer, Grant had set sail from Cork, Ireland, for Canada to serve as an aide-de-camp to Lord Elgin. Except for one year's leave of absence on private affairs, Grant held the post from October 1848 until May 1854, shortly before the completion of Elgin's eight-year tenure of office. Because Francis was such a close relative, he was no doubt treated as an intimate member of the family. Lady Elgin was an amateur artist and Francis and his aunt may well have gone sketching

16   Edward D. Nares   *Halifax*   Feb. 14, 1852

17   Edward D. Nares   *Officers at the Halifax Garrison*   Dec. 6, 1851

together from time to time. It must have been an exciting and rewarding experience for the young officer to have served in such a position of trust and responsibility with the highest official in the land. His graphic pen drawings provide us with interesting social comments on the Canadian scene at that time.

Grant seemingly left Canada shortly thereafter and went directly to the Crimea, judging by his surviving dated watercolours of Varna and other Bulgarian scenes, and Istanbul, in the National Army Museum, London. He died several months later, at the age of twenty-five, in the cholera epidemic of 1854.

The works from the second album that Baskett acquired in 1958, were done by another officer-artist, who signed his works either E.D. Nares or with the monogram E.D.N.

Edward Denne Nares was born in England in April 1831. Two years younger than Francis Grant, he was the son of a Reverend. Young Nares achieved top grades while attending public school and his family hoped he would go to Oxford. Instead he decided to seek a commission in the army, and, in 1850, he joined the 97th Foot Regiment where he served as ensign for four years.

During his posting in New Brunswick and Nova Scotia from October 1850 to November 1852, Nares worked in pen and pencil, and watercolour, sketching many views, including Halifax and environs, Fredericton, and the Bay of Fundy, and recording such activities as spearing salmon by torchlight, and moose hunting in New Brunswick. Some of his 1851 studies are of Halifax garrison soldiers in their colourful dress uniforms. Many of them took part in the social life of the town, and marriages to daughters of Halifax citizens were not uncommon, further nourishing the strong Scottish and English roots that exist in the province of Nova Scotia to this day.

Nares, having completed two years of colonial service, then obtained a year's leave of absence. Niagara Falls, a popular place to visit, was probably his destination, travelling via Boston and returning through New York City and Boston. His studies from that trip include harbour views of New York City and Boston, and the Bunker Hill monument in the latter city.

Nares' drawings, attractive and in mint condition with place names, detail, and dates, add just a little more to our knowledge of life in the Maritimes during mid-century colonial days.

18   Capt. R. Coulson   *Cape Diamond and the Plains of Abraham, Quebec,*
from Wolfe's Cove   1841

In 1980, we discovered another album in England, inscribed: "Sketches in Canada and the United States by Captn. R. Coulson, Grenr. Guards." On the inside cover, the artist had written, "Views in Canada and the United States in 1839, 1840 & 1842." The works, twenty-one in all, are in watercolour. Each painting is place-named and some are dated. These represent historic views of *Cape Diamond and the Plains of Abraham from Wolfe's Cove*, 1841; *Grand River, Ottawa, Bytown, Canada*, 1842; *L'Islet du Portage, River St. Lawrence*, 1841.

Robert Blenkinsopp Coulson was born about 1805, served in the military from 1827 to 1846, seemingly never married, and died in 1849 in Perth. He was a son of the Coulsons of Blenkinsopp Castle, Northumberland, where the Blenkinsopps had resided for centuries. Coming from a background with strong links to the army and navy, Robert purchased an ensign commission, in his case with the 98th Regiment of Foot. In 1831, he transferred to the Grenadier Guards with the rank of ensign and lieutenant and in 1836, he was promoted to captain. Coulson travelled with the 2nd Battalion from Portsmouth to Quebec, arriving in May 1839. By November, the regiment moved to Montreal due to the unrest there during the 1837 and 1838 Rebellions.

By studying Coulson's handwriting and looking at his watercolour drawings one can judge him as well-schooled with the trained eye of an artist of superior ability. His watercolours are characterized by somewhat spiky shapes but are surprisingly luminous, and possess the elements of good perspective. The details of ships, churches, and forts, and little figures in the middle distance, make his pictures enjoyable and easy to look at. His work shows the pervasive influence of Paul Sandby, the famous watercolourist and teacher, who tutored nearly two generations of aspiring young officers in landscape painting at the Royal Military Academy in Woolwich from 1768 to 1796. It has been said that Sandby was the first British artist to "infuse nature" into topographical drawing. He left the mark of his teaching genius on many a young cadet at the academy, as well as on other art students of the day who were fortunate enough to have a chance to study with him.

In May 1978, we once again heard that an album of early watercolours of British Columbia was about to be sold by auction in a small town in the English West Country. The discovery of this rare

19   Capt. R. Coulson   *Grand River, Ottawa, Bytown, Canada*   1842

item aroused much interest among dealers, museum archivists, and collectors and it was no wonder because the pre-sale publicity in the media was extensive both in England and Canada. The subjects included views of the town of Victoria from the harbour, scenes in the colony's interior with mountains, lakes, and rivers and drawings depicting mining operations during the hectic gold-rush days in the Cariboo country during the early 1860s.

We knew immediately we had to buy the album because of the rare British Columbia watercolours it contained. These drawings are certainly among the earliest art records from that part of the world except for a few topographical watercolours by Captain H.J. Warre in 1845 and some Paul Kane sketches of 1846-1848.

There was something else about the album that made it even more interesting. On nine companion pages to the watercolours appeared passages taken from a diary made during extensive trips into the British Columbia interior. There are also captions that identify nearly every picture. Unfortunately several of the drawings had been removed from the pages, leaving only the handwritten titles. One acknowledgement reads simply "Journal," and, on another page, "Bishop's Journal." These revelations, of course, added to the album's historical importance. We purchased the album in partnership with a London colleague.

A day or two after the auction, I was chatting with my partner in the office of his gallery, when in walked a professorial-looking man in rather rumpled clothes, who introduced himself in the polite manner of an English gentleman, and said he was a psychologist by profession. He also told us he had a great interest in the early history of British Columbia, and had gotten my partner's name, as the buyer of the album, from the auction house that had handled the sale. He then proceeded to remove from his worn old briefcase maps showing details of the routes of journeys taken deep into the interior of British Columbia by a certain Anglican Bishop and his party, during the days of the Cariboo gold rush. I believe he claimed himself a descendant of one of the clergymen who was active in the founding of the first Anglican diocese in British Columbia. Then after a moment's pause our visiting psychologist mentioned that he had a connection with an historical group in New

20 Edward M. Richardson *Gold Mining in the Cariboo* 1865

York who would be interested in buying the album. Although there was much interest in it, we were not at the time in a hurry to sell.

It was only some time later, after considerable research, that we discovered the identity of the bishop. He turned out to be an individual who had played an important role in establishing the Church of England in British Columbia years before that vast territory joined Canada as a province in 1871. His name was George Hills and he was the first Bishop of British Columbia, remaining there from 1859 to 1892.

This determined member of the clergy, and his associates, were not pious parsons or timid clerics. They staunchly put their faith in the ultimate power and good of God and the Church of England, the same way the army officers in peacetime strictly followed the precepts of law and order and good government. The bishop himself believed in bringing the teachings of the church to the furthest outposts of the British Columbia hinterland.

The Right Reverend George Hills was born in Kent, England, in 1816. In 1859, he was appointed bishop to the newly formed See of British Columbia in letters patent by Queen Victoria and consecrated at Westminster Abbey in an august ceremony attended by the Archbishop of Canterbury and other luminaries of the church. Before departing on his venture, which he undertook enthusiastically, but with some anxiety and trepidation, the Rev. Hills first visited every part of England to raise funds to invest in the work that lay before him.

On November 7, 1859 the Rev. George Hills left England for his diocese in British Columbia, and by mid-1860 he had settled down in Victoria. The bishop recruited junior clergymen to help him build up the church's presence in British Columbia. The Anglican clerics were well-educated men, often holding degrees from Oxford or Cambridge. The bishop, who held a master's degree from University College in Durham, was a man of energy and strong faith who also had the ability to create enthusiasm among his workers and colleagues. But it wasn't easy for him and he ran into terrible opposition both on political and religious grounds. An appalling period of financial depression hit the colony after the gold rush had petered out, creating serious problems for the bishop who had spent large sums from English endowment funds to finance the building of churches and other work in the colony. It was to take

21   Edward M. Richardson   *Williams Lake Indians*   1864

some years before life began to improve again. But Hills remained in his post for thirty-three years. History remembers him as the first and great Bishop of British Columbia.

Although not an artist himself, he appreciated the wonderful things an artist could create with his brush and he understood the value of their paintings as permanent records of remote places.

Among items in the album, then, are five colourful watercolours by the English artist-surveyor, Edward M. Richardson. Richardson uses colour in a striking manner and his meticulously painted works remind one of dream-like oriental images. One wonders whether this artist had lived in China or had studied Far Eastern art at the British Museum. Of the five watercolours in his album, three depict British Columbia Indian subjects and are dated 1864; one relates to gold mining in the Cariboo, and is dated 1865; the fifth is a view of Victoria from the harbour, dated 1864.

The album, whose cover is well worn after a period of nearly 120 years, also contained works by Edmund T. Coleman, several by R.G. Schofield, and Frederick Whymper. Other unsigned drawings were possibly by William G.R. Hind, and one suggests the hand of Edwin Porcher, an officer-artist in the service of the Royal Navy station at Esquimalt, which was within walking distance of Victoria. Coleman, Richardson, and Whymper were professionally trained English artists who travelled to Victoria around 1860, looking for possible employment as artists with expeditions exploring the interior of Vancouver Island or the mainland. Some of them perhaps dreamed of striking it rich by finding gold in the auriferous gravel of some swift-running stream in the remote Cariboo.

One of the watercolours in the album is a faithful depiction of the Christ Church Cathedral in Victoria, before it was destroyed by fire and rebuilt, and a modest house nearby called the bishop's cottage, painted by E.T. Coleman in 1863. As well as being an artist, Coleman was an experienced mountain climber who wrote illustrated articles in mountaineering. Apparently he remained in British Columbia from about 1860 to 1870, as his name appears in the press as artist resident, from time to time.

Throughout the years relatively few paintings of British Columbia subject matter have come into our possession, and few I can think of were executed before those of the late 1880s by the Canadian Pacific Railway artists. Cut off by the Rocky Mountains until

22   R.G. Schofield   *Antler Creek, Cariboo*   March 1863

the CPR was completed in 1885, British Columbia had little communication with eastern British North America in the early days.

The bishop learned much about the geography of the country from his trips, was precise in the points of the compass, and knew the direction and flow of the great rivers. The bishop kept a daily diary for the final thirty-five years of his life, and for our story the most interesting and revealing entries record his trips into the interior of British Columbia in 1860, 1861, and 1862, covering distances up to 1189 miles in a season. The following is an entry from the album, quoting from Hills' diaries, dated May 31, 1860, Harrison Lake, and reveals the bishop's keen interest and outlook during his first trip into the interior.

"The greater part of our course lay through a magnificent Lake – the Harrison – reminding me of Loch Ness but upon a larger scale. The mountains on either side are of considerable height and water falls and cascades frequent."

An excerpt from the July 21, 1862 entry continues opposite a blank space where originally there had been a watercolour of the *Fraser, at the Junction of the Quesnelle.* He describes the river being negotiated by their pack horses swimming across. "The river being rapid they were carried down some way by the current. It was curious to watch the 10 heads all above water with pricked ears and snorting noses pressing for the opposite shore."

An entry on the page opposite a watercolour of the *Bald Mountain Cariboo*, reads: "The air was fine, bracing & invigorating without being in the least degree cold. Indeed there was a balminess like the early morn of hay time in England. The mountain prospect was magnificent."

It was into the Victoria of 1871 that the legendary painter Emily Carr was born, and there is little doubt that Bishop Hills was well acquainted with Emily's father, Richard Carr, a prominent Victoria merchant and pillar of the church at the time. Mrs. Edward Cridge, wife of the contentious dean of Christ Church Cathedral, taught some of the Carr children, including Emily, at Sunday School.

A neatly packaged little story would have been the result if we could have concluded that the bishop himself had put together the album, but the handwriting is not his. The descriptive passages in the album are excerpts, with minor variations, from Hills' diaries

23   R.G. Schofield   *The Bald Mountain, Cariboo*   March 1863

today in possession of the Archives of the Anglican Provincial Synod of British Columbia, Vancouver. It is known that at least two of the artists, Whymper and Richardson, made available copies of their paintings to anyone who wished to purchase them and it is on record that Whymper sold watercolours to the Anglican clerics, Sheepshanks, R.C.L. Brown, and H.P. Wright during this period.

It is reasonable to suggest that the album was created by someone who knew the bishop well enough to gain access to his diaries and perhaps to some of his art and who possibly had accompanied him on at least one of those three memorable trips. Handwriting specimens of several close associates of Hills were located for comparison to that in the album but all were ruled out. As a result we may never discover the name of the actual person who, with much loving care, put together this fascinating album.

24 Emily Carr *Gitwangak, Queen Charlotte Islands* 1912

25   James W. Morrice   *A Brittany Girl*   c.1902

4

Drawings and Other Works from Canada's Early Days

A drawing is an illusion, the volume and reality of its subject filled in by the mind's eye. I think of drawing as a language all its own and sometimes even though slight, a drawing can take its place as a work of art, and a statement of truth. The urge to draw has always been a dominant feature in mankind, and a form of communication with its roots reaching deep into antiquity.

My own special interest in drawings goes back a long time, first awakened, I believe, on seeing reproductions of black and white drawings by Vincent van Gogh during the early 1930s. These were produced by the Munich fine art publishers, Piper and Company, and our firm had imported a portfolio of them to try and sell in Toronto. These facsimiles were the same size as the originals and printed on toned paper that looked, even on close examination, as though they were indeed the real thing.

Another artist whose drawings kindled a positive response in me was Rembrandt. I began to know his black and white works by looking at reproductions of his drawings and etchings in books, and later I was fortunate in seeing many of his originals in English and

European collections. When you gaze at his little brown pen drawings, your eye is immediately aware that there is something special and monumental about them – it is then you begin to realize that his art is timeless. Drawings he made three and a half centuries ago, except for the costumes of the period, which date them precisely, can appear as rich and eloquent as if they were done yesterday.

Rembrandt's compatriot, Vincent van Gogh, two and a half centuries later, possessed the same dynamic thrust for expressing himself, and in his own way was just as great an artist. With his stubby quill pen, van Gogh created drawings of such emotional power that they literally stunned his friends and contemporaries. Van Gogh was as well a sensitive and expressive letter writer and over the years poured out his feelings on life and art to his brother Theo, and often drew on the edge of the pages little pen sketches to illustrate his ideas for paintings. When you become involved with the art of van Gogh you are vicariously caught in his struggle to impose himself, body and soul, over nature. That's why he created his gnarled and twisted cypress trees, his cawing, cawing crows in tortuous flight over storm-blown corn fields.

I believe it was the study of the art of these two Dutchmen, along with lesser artists that contributed to my appreciation of good drawings and finally stimulated my interest in Canada's important legacy of drawings and watercolours from the nineteenth century.

Our country did indeed possess a few artists of great merit during this period. These included the British military and naval officers to whom I devoted the previous chapter. Some of them were excellent artists, map-makers, and topographers, who produced drawings and watercolours of the first rank. Fortunately many of these watercolours have survived and provide us with a varied and sometimes colourful look at British North America from 1759 until Confederation.

With the exception of a handful of native-born artists, such as the Quebeckers, Antoine Plamondon (1804-1895) and his pupil Théophile Hamel (1817-1870), and newly arrived immigrants like William Berczy (who came to Upper Canada in 1794), professional resident artists were few and far between in Canada's sparse population. We are therefore indebted to the legacy of work left by these enthusiastic amateurs from the British forces, who, when their tour of duty in Canada was over, returned to England or Scotland with

26   William Berczy   *Portrait of a Nobleman*   c.1785

28 Frederick A. Verner *The Sentinel* 1874

27 Frederick A. Verner *A Young Indian Chief* 1871

sketch books filled with drawings and watercolours of their personal observations, some accompanied by written comments on the Canadian scene.

I have to remind myself constantly that it was not until some sixteen years ago, in 1966, that buyers of Canadian art, few as they were at the time, expressed any interest in drawings or watercolours by the artists of Canada's earlier days. In fact they were generally spurned by prospective buyers as trivialities, and most people didn't even take the trouble to look at them. Attitudes and tastes having completely changed, and there is now an avid interest in Canadiana of every description. This new respect for the art of our past is growing steadily.

One of the more disparaged and misunderstood characters of Upper Canada's late eighteenth century, who is now receiving a belated but warm recognition, was the Saxony-born artist-colonizer and talented miniature painter William Berczy (1748-1813). According to his biographer, John André, Berczy's talents were varied and his accomplishments many. As well as being a cultured scholar, he was exceedingly well trained in the art of painting, and was Upper Canada's finest artist of his time. André also points out that William Berczy should enjoy an equal status with Governor John Graves Simcoe as a co-founder of Toronto (actually York, as it was known until 1834). He was responsible for much of the building of Yonge Street and the downtown area, designing the first bridge to cross the Don River and some of York's finest houses.

Some Canadian history books downgrade Berczy as a somewhat disreputable entrepreneur, a land developer who because of inexcusable delays lost a government contract to create a settlement on 64,000 acres in Markham Township with immigrants from Germany. Although the settlement flourished briefly, legal problems cropped up and the land grant was cancelled. All this happened nearly 200 years ago. This year, 1982, the city of Toronto is finally honouring the Berczy name, and is planning to erect a statue of him in bronze to be placed in a downtown park dedicated to his memory.

Berczy's most famous painting is the 1809 Montreal-commissioned work featuring the Woolsey family. It is a composition with eight figures and a dog. However, he is also known for his excellent studies of the Six Nations chief, Joseph Brant, and the

29   Charles J. Way   *View of Quebec from the River Marshes*   c.1880

30   F. McGillivray Knowies   *A Quiet Ontario Village*   1897

colourful miniature portraits he created during the final quarter of the eighteenth century.

During the years between 1935 and 1982, our firm acquired in Britain alone possibly as many as 4,000 early colour prints and engravings, watercolours and pen and pencil drawings in sketch books and paintings, all of Canadian interest. Some were found intact in their original albums and the dates spanned the years of nearly three-quarters of the last century. During trips to Paris, the centre of the French art world, I never failed to look for items pertaining to New France. But except for the occasional old print and one or two crude early portraits it was mainly a futile search. We found few works either in France or in Canada of the French colonial period.

As I reflect now on the wide gulf separating French and English attitudes toward painting and sculpture in the New World, the different points of view become striking. The arts of New France were centred largely around carvings of religious themes and flamboyantly handsome altar pieces. The Roman Catholic hierarchy religiously stressed the Christian heritage of the old land. Polychromed madonnas and heavenly angels were later created by Quebec-born wood sculptors, thus embodying the French sense of the palpable and three-dimensional side of life. On the other hand, the well-trained British topographers' output was entirely two-dimensional and secular.

The earliest Canadian topographical watercolour I recall handling was in the mid-1930s, when a little watercolour by Mrs. Simcoe, wife of Governor John Graves Simcoe, came into our hands. It was a view of the Don River, possibly sketched from the garden of the Simcoes' summer residence at Castle Frank about 1795. I can also recall another small watercolour we had depicting the shore line of Lake Ontario, near the mouth of the Humber River, by Elizabeth Frances Hale, signed and dated 1802. At the time Mrs. Hale's husband was paymaster general for the British forces in Canada. These were handed to us by our next-door bookseller friend, Roy Britnell, whose family for many years has operated one of Canada's finest bookshops. From time to time while buying up old libraries in private houses, Roy would find Canadian drawings and pictures that he would quietly turn over to us.

In the 1930s, scores of excellent watercolours of the nine-

31 J.B. Wilkinson *Icebound on the St. Lawrence* 1878

32 Henry Sandham *Lake Scene with Mountains* c.1880

33   J.M. Barnsley   *An East Coast Fishing Village*   1889

teenth-century Canadian school appeared on the market. Many old Toronto families, who owned houses in the Annex and later built in fashionable Rosedale, had adorned their walls with these pictures. In fact, by about 1910, such watercolours had become quite popular with middle-class Torontonians who took great pride in decorating their houses with them. After all, they were quite reasonable, at prices ranging from $25 to $150. Twenty years later they began to lose their popular appeal, however, and went straight out of fashion. People just stored them away in their basements or attics, and local auctioneers, such as Henderson's in Toronto, offered them in their house sales.

Throughout the 1930s and even into the 1950s household furnishings from estates were often auctioned off on the premises piecemeal, room by room, but even though we bought these pictures at the most modest of prices, they were extremely difficult to resell. There was little interest in the watercolour medium because the surface needed glass for protection and people disliked the reflection that often distorted the look of the picture. In addition, the newly built houses of the time had large clear glass windows that let in strong sunlight, and the watercolours, with their old-fashioned wide gilt mats and ornate frames, just looked completely out of place in these bright rooms hanging on the fashionable pastel-coloured walls. But in spite of selling difficulties, my father, a man of strong and positive nature, liked this style of painting and vowed that the whole nineteenth-century Canadian watercolour school would one day be reassessed and much sought after again. His prediction turned out to be correct. In the meantime, our collection of attractive but difficult-to-sell watercolours, continued to increase in numbers.

One of the artists we collected was Frederick A. Verner. His splendid watercolours of Indians found their way into many Victorian parlours of Toronto's well-to-do, and made them look respectable.

Born in the little hamlet of Sheridon, Ontario in 1836, Verner was one of Upper Canada's earliest native-born artists. Also he was probably the most popular and prolific of our nineteenth-century watercolourists, though earlier in his career he painted some important oil portraits on canvas. These included an 1871 study of a young Indian chief, the subject in full tribal costume pos-

34   Frederic M. Bell-Smith   *A Thames Bridge, London*   c.1897

ing with great dignity and pride. His favourite themes were Indian encampments, and lake scenes with Indians paddling or portaging their magnificent birch-bark canoes. Verner delighted in painting these canoes and considered them one of the Indians' finest art forms. Other subjects were scenes of the western buffalo quietly grazing and once in a while a herd stampeding before a prairie fire. In winter he painted them foraging for food in deep snow.

Verner made his first far western journey in 1862, when he was twenty-six years old. He also travelled West in 1867, 1870, and 1873 proceeding by Red River cart, canoe, and on horseback. Like his artist hero Paul Kane, whose portrait he later painted, Verner was a strong, robust man who thrived on those early trips, producing sketch material that he would use over and over again during his long painting life. In spite of his extensive travels in the West, though, I have never seen a Verner painting of a buffalo subject that could match the dynamism of Paul Kane's spellbinding buffalo hunts, eye-witness renditions of the Métis charging the animals on horseback or trapping them in a pound. One reason, perhaps, is that by the time of Verner's first western trip in 1862, the buffalo population had been drastically reduced. The reckless and colourful hunts that Kane described and painted so brilliantly in 1846 were things of the past. Nor, I feel, was Verner endowed with Kane's great insight and painting talents. It is interesting to note that in the 1930s and 1940s pictures featuring Indians were particularly difficult to sell. Some of our important mining clients actively disliked them and wouldn't dream of taking home a painting featuring an Indian. This prejudice was probably related to earlier contacts with Indians during their mineral prospecting days in the northern bush.

As Verner got older the quality of his work deteriorated and his watercolours became fuzzy and the faces of his Indian subjects vague and lifeless. When he retired to England to live out the final years of his long life, he made many English landscapes but frequently painted from memory the Canadian Indian themes he knew so well from the days of his youth.

For years we continued to accumulate the works of Frederick Verner and added to our collection a further thirty watercolours in 1958, when we bought out William Watson's collection just before his retirement from the picture business in Montreal. Finally, in

35   Frederic M. Bell-Smith   *A Camp in the Rockies*   1889

1967, we held a catalogued Canadian Centennial exhibition of thirty-seven Verner watercolours, all of which were for sale at prices from $300 to $3,000. This was certainly the most important showing of Verner's work held during the past sixty years and it attracted a large number of visitors.

We constantly added to our stock of nineteenth-century drawings and watercolours and, by the late 1950s, possessed the largest private collection in Canada. This, however, was long before the work of these artists was of interest to the art-buying public. Most of the pictures were scenes of rural Ontario, Quebec and the Maritime Provinces. Nearly all of these artists had found the time and saved up the money to study abroad, and it was all very normal that the artist should come under the pervasive influence of the French-Barbizon and Dutch-Hague Schools. Studying abroad was beneficial and they profited from the instruction. Their production forms an important part of all the art that Canada possessed in those days and, looking back at them now, these works awaken a genuine nostalgia for rural Canada – seen without the cynical eye of the 1980s.

Some of the artists to whom I refer are F. McGillivray Knowles, Laura Muntz, James Barnsley, T. Mower-Martin, W. St. Thomas Smith, Marmaduke Matthews, C.M. Manley, Henry Sandham, Charles J. Way, William Cresswell and Robert Holmes, to name only a few. My favourite is the last named who painted wonderful wildflower studies. All of these painters had roots deep in the nineteenth century. Along with the artists mentioned we also bought a large collection of watercolours from the estate of Robert Gagen, who had studied under Mr. Cresswell. These watercolours bring back a forgotten quality of peace and pleasure into our hectic modern lives.

Another important watercolourist of the nineteenth century was F.M. Bell-Smith, drawing master, amateur actor, and poet. He, like Verner, had a large following during his lifetime. We must have accumulated more than 100 of his watercolours painted from the mid-1870s onwards. These included paintings made during 1887, on his first trip by rail to the Rocky Mountains, and later street scenes of London, featuring landmark subjects like the Parliament Buildings, Fleet Street, and Thames bridges. In Paris he painted romantic subjects such as the Tuileries Rue Royale, and

36   Edward Roper   *A North West Coast Indian Village*   c.1880

37   Daniel Fowler   *Landscape, Amherst Island*   1887

38 Daniel Fowler *Game Birds – Still Life* 1869

the Madeleine.

Bell-Smith's trips through the Rocky Mountains in the late eighties were made possible through the good offices of Sir William Van Horne, the art-loving president of the CPR. Sir William was probably Canada's earliest collector of Old Masters and reputed to have the finest collection of Spanish masters outside of Spain. He also bought work by the French Impressionists. He painted landscapes himself as a hobby, but his painting skills could not match his shrewd intellect nor his good taste in buying other forms of art. He would have enjoyed a good laugh to learn that sixty-five years after his demise, a collection of his own work would sell for a large sum of money and would be hanging in the Toronto head office of a major international oil company.

Another accomplished watercolourist was Daniel Fowler, who came to Canada from England in 1843, already a well-trained artist of thirty-three. But instead of continuing his painting career, he became a farmer, buying a 100-acre farm on flat and productive Amherst Island situated near eastern Ontario's Bay of Quinte. Since he had to support a family, and there was no sale for pictures, for nearly fourteen years he didn't put a brush to paper. Then, for no apparent reason, he got the urge to paint again and produced some wonderfully lyrical landscapes near his island home and some still life wild game subjects that are among the best works produced in the late nineteenth-century Canada. These game birds were sought after in many rural areas of southeastern Ontario as a source of food. Dead game, perhaps, which would later wind up tasty dishes at the dinner table, but the artist treated his subject with consummate understanding and sensitivity. He succeeded beautifully in capturing some of the elusive texture and iridescent hues of their plummage.

We also liked the watercolours of William Armstrong, particularly his Great Lakes shipping and Indian encampment subjects. Born in County Cork, Ireland, he came to Canada in 1851, at the age of nineteen. Armstrong was a prodigious worker, both as an artist and an engineer. He painted a large number of watercolours during a long and productive life, including scenes of Toronto Bay in summer and winter, events at the Royal Canadian Yacht Club, and harbours and ships of the lakes as far west as the Port Arthur district, where he temporarily lived. Later he became a well-known

39 William Armstrong   *Squaw Plucking Ducks Near Fort William,*
Lake Superior   1865

figure in Toronto and was art instructor at the Normal-Model School. Armstrong actively painted around the Great Lakes more than fifty years before Group of Seven members discovered Algoma. His large watercolour of the last distribution of the government bounty to the Indians at Great Manitoulin Island, Canada West, is a mid-nineteenth-century cultural and artistic masterpiece, depicting some sixty-five figures in movement or repose. Armstrong's name would be remembered for this one work alone.

Like William Armstrong, many of these nineteenth-century artists were fortunate to hold teaching posts in private Canadian schools to help eke out a half-decent living for themselves. Upper Canada College, Ridley, the Ontario Ladies College, Moulton, and Alma College in St. Thomas, were among the schools that boasted having professional artists on their teaching staff. It is currently chic to brand these schools as merely elite; the fact is they provided a stability and cultural tradition that was unique, and our society is much the better for them.

One of the most talented Canadian-born artists of the last century, whose work we were always searching for, was Lucius O'Brien, born in Shanty Bay, Canada West, in 1832. He was a book illustrator of distinction and like other of his contemporaries was constantly on the move all over Canada, including trips to paint the Ottawa River and its tributaries, and during the late 1880s the Rocky Mountains as one of the CPR artists. His watercolours are luminous with an out-of-doors freshness that make them a delight to look at.

In September 1966, the Laing Galleries held an exhibition entitled "Canada of the Nineteenth Century in Watercolours." It featured the work of nearly all the artists we have mentioned, including some from the British-officer school, as well as some unidentified topographers. In all, there were 107 pieces on view. There were a few well-known names included, but what I found interesting was the immense geographical scope the exhibition covered: the Maritimes, Quebec, Ontario and the far West. Such an exhibition and sale today would create great interest in the art market but, in 1966, sales were insignificant.

Another nineteenth-century-born Canadian was LeMoine FitzGerald, and it gives me a feeling of satisfaction to end this chapter with the remarkable FitzGerald acquisition. Just over twenty

40 William Armstrong *Indians in War Canoes* 1877

41 Blair Bruce *A Summer Day in Normandy* c.1890

42   Homer Watson   *A Passing Storm, Doon*   1885

years ago, in the autumn of 1961, a chubby man, his face brimming with smiles, head topped with a black sombrero and wearing highly polished Mexican boots, walked into our gallery. He carried a thin, rectangular parcel under his arm and said his name was Edward FitzGerald. His face seemed somehow familiar but I couldn't recall the circumstances of when or where I had seen him before. Then, in a flash it all came back. His face was exactly the face of his father, the artist LeMoine FitzGerald. I had never met the elder FitzGerald in person, but had seen a photograph of him reproduced in the catalogue of his 1958 memorial exhibition. Also I had visited the artist's widow at her home in Winnipeg and recalled seeing photographs of her late husband on those occasions.

Edward FitzGerald then removed the paper from the package he was carrying and I was not altogether surprised when he produced a small attractive unframed panel by his artist father, depicting two luscious red apples lying on a table. I bought the picture immediately and on that very same day sold it to my Edmonton friend, H.R. Milner. It is now a part of the Milner estate collection on loan to the Edmonton Art Gallery. Edward went on to tell me that he had inherited a large collection of his father's work, black and white and coloured drawings, some watercolours, and a few small oils, which were in Mexico, where he was then living. He immediately piqued my interest.

At this time, I left for Winnipeg and the West Coast with a collection of pictures for exhibition and sale. Shortly after my arrival in Winnipeg, FitzGerald telephoned from Mexico City inviting me to come down and look at a collection of his father's drawings he wished to dispose of. About two weeks passed and then my wife, who had accompanied me on the trip, and I, flew from Vancouver to Mexico City. We were met at the airport by Edward, again sporting his Mexican outfit, who brought us in his grand chauffeur-driven car, which he had rented for the occasion, to the Mexico City Hilton Hotel.

I remember to this day how tired I was after the flight from Vancouver to Mexico City, not realizing at the time that it was the high altitude and thin atmosphere that were taking their toll. After a rest, and feeling better, we later drove around town visiting the museum of Aztec art and viewing some of Diego Rivera's great murals. Like everyone else who has been to Mexico, I was struck by

43   Lucius R. O'Brien   *Fishing Near the Ottawa River*   1875

the contrast of wealth and poverty. All together in the central part of the city there were Spanish neo-Mannerist mansions, with their high walls and teams of servants, and nearby those wretched tin and cardboard hovels.

The next afternoon Edward brought to the hotel several bulging portfolios of his father's work, each containing unframed drawings and watercolours. It didn't take long for us to agree on a price for some 300 works of art. There were all sorts of subjects, including interiors and still lifes, landscapes and nude studies from the 1920s up to the early 1950s. The following day, Edward manoeuvred us through the intricacies of Mexican customs and we were able to leave the country accompanied by portfolios of our precious pictures.

The Edward FitzGerald that I got to know was an unusual individual. Artistic like his father, he was also an idealist and a visionary, usually needing money for special causes he and his wife Paula were promoting. They belonged to some kind of Christian brotherhood group. Fitz, as he was known, was content to live a life of simple tastes, except on occasions when he wanted to display his own special brand of sophistication.

When we purchased the LeMoine FitzGerald collection from Edward on that occasion in Mexico City, we regarded it as an important acquisition, both because of the large number of pictures involved and the fine quality of the work. It was a long-term investment and today, twenty years later, we still have on hand some drawings from the original hoard. Though practically unknown at the time, FitzGerald has now emerged as one of Canada's distinguished twentieth-century artists.

44 LeMoine FitzGerald   *A Farm at Snowflake, Manitoba*   c.1930

45 Frederick H. Varley *A Flanders Battlefield* 1918

5

The Purloined Rembrandt

For about two years in the late 1920s, a certain A. Luscombe Carroll was manager of the T. Eaton Company's fine art department. He was formerly a picture dealer from London who became a resident of Toronto, and imported traditional English and European nineteenth-century oil paintings by the hundreds, which were then placed on exhibition and sale at Eaton's. Most of these were supplied by his father who operated a small commercial gallery in London.

A. Luscombe Carroll was born with a combination of bravura and brazen confidence and even during the worst days of the mid-1930s, when nothing at all was selling, he remained optimistic. He had met with reasonable success during the prosperous years of the late 1920s when it was relatively easy to sell European pictures and so felt no doubt that better days would soon return. However, he persisted in luxuriating in the grand manner, and he moved to a Forest Hill mansion, continuing to spend more money than he could possibly earn. He wore natty clothes, possessed a large, shiny bald head, a ruddy complexion, and exuded a pompous manner. But he worked diligently at picture dealing and travelled frequently throughout the country, holding small exhibitions of rather mediocre pictures and inexpensive watercolours, the latter by three of his favourite English artists: John Charles Collings, A. Winter-Shaw, and N.H.J. Baird. I still think of him as a renegade, but in the thirties I expect he was just another one of those hungry picture salesmen trying his best to survive. During the hard times when nothing was selling one of his sayings was, "You know it's too bad, but you can't eat pictures."

Carroll was constantly borrowing pictures for his exhibitions and auction sales, especially from dealer colleagues in England. Unfortunately he didn't always pay up after sales, tendering instead promissory notes which remained unpaid long after their due dates. I know of one London dealer still in business, who suffered from the results of these unfulfilled promises, and to this day more than forty years later still feels bitter about Carroll's rude treatment of him.

The most sensational art happening of Bert Carroll's life, although it turned out later to be an ill-fated one, was his purchase at Christie's London auction rooms in May 1928 of Rembrandt van Rijn's famous painting, *Lady with a Handkerchief*. Purchased with T. Eaton company funds, the cost was 30,000 golden guineas, which was then considered a staggering sum to pay out for a picture, even the work of a great master. (Converted into today's currency, allowing for inflation, the amount would surely be well over the $3,000,000 mark.) Sensing the publicity and prestige that would cling to his name in the heady world of Old Master art dealing, Carroll regarded the purchase of the portrait as a personal triumph. He would prove to all concerned that he could successfully compete with international houses like P. & D. Colnaghi and Thomas Agnew & Sons in London or M. Knoedler of New York.

The London offices of the T. Eaton Company, though mightily astonished at the huge sum involved, nevertheless took a good look at the invoice and, everything seeming in order, they paid up at once. Almost immediately the portrait was picked up by the T. Rogers Company, trusted fine art packers to royalty, carefully packed in the waterproof case, and placed on an ocean liner bound for Canada. Later it was unveiled at Eaton's Toronto store amidst considerable fanfare.

It was still a lot of money, even for the rich T. Eaton Company, and it wasn't long before eyebrows were raised among certain of the company's top brass, ignoring its potential advertising value, and indeed questioning the wisdom of such a purchase at all. They concluded that Mr. Carroll's enthusiasm had far outweighed his good judgement in spending that kind of money and it wasn't very long before Carroll left his position at Eaton's and opened up his own picture gallery in Toronto.

Meanwhile the painting remained at Eaton's and soon, with the onset of the Great Depression, any possibility of selling it faded into oblivion. To put it mildly, this magnificent white elephant with its high carrying charges was a source of acute embarrassment to Eaton's accounting department. For nearly ten years the painting languished away at their College Street store. As a visitor during the early and mid-thirties, I was privileged to view it from time to time. The portrait was enshrined in a little private showing room. Artfully lighted, it hung majestically against a background of dark velvet drapes.

Because of his grand purchase, Carroll suddenly became a high flyer in the art world, and it was going to be extremely difficult for him to settle down again to the ordinary picture business. However as easy as it is in retrospect to criticize his poor judgement, Carroll had found himself completely carried away by the excitement of an incredibly fast moving auction sale drama. He was absolutely convinced that he had bought a great work of art, and in this respect one has to admire the brash spirit and sheer audacity of the man. True, he was not spending his own money, but to contemplate buying the portrait for such a price, even though it was on behalf of the company that employed him, must have required courage, unmitigated gall, or both. In fact, he felt that he deserved special credit for bringing the picture to Canada in the first place. But that was a recognition that would never, ever, come his way.

This expensive Rembrandt portrait was from the estate of Sir George Lindsay Holford. Another picture I know well from the Holford sale is Peter Paul Rubens' *Elevation of the Cross*, bought with uncanny perspicacity by the Art Gallery of Toronto for 5,200 guineas, using the services of Alec Martin, an employee of Christie's, whom I knew later as Sir Alec, chairman of the famous art auction house. The Rubens is now considered one of the finest Old Masters in the Art Gallery of Ontario and among the few genuine works by the great Flemish master in Canada.

A third painting from the Holford sale, and one we once

owned, was *Travellers Before an Inn* by Karel du Jardin. The story of my discovery of this work during a trip to Cuba in 1967 is related in my previous book. The du Jardin is recorded as having belonged to the Holford family as early as 1854 by the German art historian scholar Dr. Waagen, then director of the Royal Gallery, Berlin. Dr. Waagen spent many months recording Old Masters in English collections before publishing his celebrated catalogue on the "Treasures of Art in Great Britain." He described the du Jardin at the time as "a picture of unusual power and freshness," a description that still holds good today.

Luscombe Carroll's purchase of the Rembrandt must have captured my imagination and I wanted to learn more about the Holford collection. On many occasions I had seen references to the Holford pictures in catalogues and art publications, and my knowledgeable auctioneer friend, John Lumley of Christie's, suggested the Westminster Library in London as the best source of further information. In June 1981 I visited the library, housed in a lovely Georgian building at the rear of the National Gallery. There I found all the background material I needed to satisfy my curiosity about the family's history.

I soon discovered that it was not Col. George Lindsay Holford who had assembled the collection but rather his father, Robert Staynor Holford aided by the advice of art dealer William Buchanan. George's grandfather was governor of the New River Company which distributed London's fresh water supply. It was through this lucrative monopoly that the Holford family became rich by the end of the eighteenth century, and by the beginning of the nineteenth century, immensely so. As a young man Robert Holford inherited a million pounds from a bachelor uncle and then more millions from his father, as an only son. He was a solid Victorian member of a country-based family whose life spanned eighty-four years of the nineteenth century.

The inheritance of such enormous wealth made it possible for Robert Holford to achieve his ambition of building two great houses that he perceived "would be different." It was in Dorchester House in London, and Westonbrit in the Cotswolds that he showed off his collection of Old Master paintings by artists of the Italian, Spanish, Flemish, Dutch and other schools. Imagine it! He owned five Rembrandts and also had a near perfect collection of the master's etchings.

When his father died in 1892, Colonel George Holford inherited both the houses and the paintings. But he was not the builder or art collector that his father had been. Instead his heart was in the army, and he led the exalted life of a high-ranking officer in the service of royalty.

The T. Eaton Company always had great expectations for the success of its picture department, as much for the store's general prestige as for potential profit. Over the years they had many excellent exhibitions and showed the work of Canadian artists, including some of the best, such as J.W. Beatty, F.H. Varley, and F.H. (Franz) Johnston. But their main thrust continued to be the showing of European paintings. Eaton's ambitious plans for the future of their gallery were never quite realized, however, mainly because they were unable to project the personal image that a resourceful and progressive private gallery could attain.

Since it had been utterly impossible to sell the Rembrandt, the company directors eventually found a perfect and pragmatic solution for the future of the aristocratic lady. They decided, in December 1942, to present the portrait as a gift to the retiring president of the company, Robert Y. Eaton.

The R.Y. Eatons lived in a splendid house in Rosedale and had an eminently suitable spot to show off the picture, and the honourable Dutch lady hung with easy grace on the wall by herself in the high-ceilinged music room.

Robert Young Eaton, an honorary Lt. Colonel of the Governor General's Horse Guards, and proud of his military title, was, in fact, a shy and diffident man. As president of Eaton's in the 1930s, he had the uneviable task of guiding the business through a prolonged and serious depression. When R.Y., as he was known, died in 1956, our gallery was requested by the Eaton family to make a valuation on the Rembrandt painting, for estate purposes. In consultation with our English colleagues, the Colnaghi firm of London, recognized as the supreme authorities on the value and authenticity of works by Rembrandt, a valuation was made on October 26, 1956, of $190,000.

Lady with a Handkerchief was then turned over to the Art Gallery of Toronto as an Eaton bequest. The picture remained on view for many years as one of the institution's most admired and precious possessions, except when it was purloined and disappeared for a time off the gallery's walls, having been cut out of its frame by thieves hoping to raise ransom money. Later the shocked lady was recovered, soon restored to her former health, and returned to her place of honour in the gallery. The estate was allowed no tax deduction on this extraordinarily generous bequest and the valuation reflects the low prices that still prevailed in the international art market.

In March of 1981 I visited the Art Gallery of Ontario, expecting to have another look at the Rembrandt I had been writing about, but when I asked an attendant where it was displayed he claimed to know nothing at all about the portrait. I then talked with one of the senior curators who promised he would try and resolve the mystery. I was astounded when a little later I was told that the portrait had been removed from the gallery walls as it was no longer considered by the experts to be by the hand of Rembrandt. An optimistic opinion might be that it belonged to the "School of Rembrandt." Also they said it was now in the process of being deaccessioned, which means selling or otherwise disposing of a work from the permanent collection of an institution (a euphemism coined by museum curators to make the process of getting rid of an object sound a little better).

Lady with a Handkerchief, the likeness of a Madame Sylvius, painted about 1645, was well documented with impressive and scholarly credentials. It had also been widely exhibited during a period of a century or more in England and continental Europe, including a Rembrandt exhibition in Amsterdam in 1898. In addition it was illustrated and recorded in almost every known book on Rembrandt. No stigma or shadow of doubt had ever been raised concerning its authenticity.

One morning, two months later, I was escorted to the basement storage area of a local auction house by one of the employees to look at some Canadian pictures coming up for sale later on in the month. I could hardly believe my eyes when I saw, propped against a wall, the Holford-Carroll-Eaton Rembrandt. To make things worse the picture had been placed in a cheap and shoddy frame with no nameplate or identification whatever.

As I related the story to my companion, a Montreal dealer, I noticed an auction house employee was standing nearby listening

46   Frank H. Johnston   *The Lake at Hubert, 96 Miles North of Sault Ste. Marie*
September 1918

in wide-eyed astonishment. The employee finally admitted that the painting was in the process of being catalogued by Miss X for their next non-Canadian picture auction. The portrait, having fallen from grace, was about to be sold by the Art Gallery of Ontario, apparently without the permission of the donor's family.

I remember thinking to myself what an unworthy fate for a great portrait and that it would likely just slip through a Toronto auction sale with the story of its astonishing history untold. It would doubtless be listed as "Dutch School" and I even had visions of buying it myself, or calling in a London-based partner to buy it together in shares. There was no hurry for a decision on the matter because the picture would have to be catalogued, and since we received all sales notices from the auctioneers, we would know in good time the date of the sale.

I must confess that when I saw the portrait in its cheap frame there in that storeroom, standing amidst a confusion of trashy objects, it didn't look nearly as regal as I had remembered it. It had lost much of its glamour and appeal. I have experienced before a loss of confidence in a painting. Once, in particular, I felt shaken when I bought what looked like a superb small racing scene by Edgar Degas and which later proved to be a fake. It does happen that once the authenticity of a work you have admired and believed in comes under a cloud of suspicion, the picture or object described as doubtful will never again look the same in your eyes. It is a strange and powerful emotion. Nevertheless I felt outraged at finding my beloved grand dame in the trash bin, so to speak.

A day or so after this extraordinary incident I related my story to a confidant at the Art Gallery of Ontario. Another four weeks passed and on June 18, when I had returned to Toronto from a business trip to Europe, I went to the Art Gallery to meet a friend. Since I was a little early for my engagement, I decided to take a walk through the Old Master section of the gallery. Another big shock followed, but this time it was a pleasant one. I had suddenly come face to face with my revered lady, once again serenely hanging on the gallery walls, and back in the seventeenth-century jet black frame that so suited her. I must say she once again looked resplendent. There was now, however, a small printed card nearby on the wall which read, "Rembrandt School." But, she seemed content to be home again, for I think I detected a small glimmer of a smile on her face.

During the last few years, teams of art historians have been studying the seventeenth-century art of the Netherlands and Rembrandt's work in particular. Using what they describe as modern techniques and historical methods they have been working their way through art museums and other institutions possessing works by Rembrandt and other Old Masters, trying to weed out the copies and "school" studies and in so doing debunking many pictures formerly recognized as being by a master's hand. Apparently some of these historians decided the *Lady with a Handkerchief* was one of those "school" pictures. However, a pendulum swings both ways. I wouldn't therefore be surprised if other experts come along during the next thirty years or so, and the grand old dame, Madame Sylvius, is once again returned to her former state of glory, completely recovering her status as a Rembrandt masterpiece.

47   David B. Milne   *Two Maples, Palgrave*   1932

6

Some Artists and Collectors in the Thirties

In 1934, within two years following the establishment of our gallery, my father, who by now was spending his full time at the business, began to consider the possibilities of promoting the sale of Canadian art. Although a market was almost non-existent at the time, he soon had me looking around for some native Canadian talent. Our new gallery was ideally situated in the Yonge-Bloor area and several artists lived or had studios within a five-minute walking radius of the gallery.

There were, for instance, the portrait and flower painter Archibald Barnes, and Arthur Heming, whose romantic animal subjects touched the heart of the dearest Canadian clichés, and Tom Stone, a hopeful landscape artist. Also nearby in the Studio Building there were the artists George and Kathleen Pepper, Curtis Williamson, and Thoreau MacDonald. The building also included as tenants, J.W. Beatty, A.Y. Jackson and Lawren Harris (Harris and Dr. James MacCallum having shared the cost of its construction some twenty years before), these three now recognized as giants among our landscape painters.

I remember one of our artist neighbours, Tom Stone, a man with jet-black hair and trim moustache, who was very debonair. He, in fact, reminded me in looks of the movie star, John Gilbert,

Garbo's leading man. Stone had a small studio flat in a building next door to the old Yorkville Town Hall on Yonge Street. He priced his small winter scenes at $20 apiece and still no one wanted them. It's a mystery to me how Tom Stone ever survived those lean and hungry years.

Nineteen-thirty-four was also the memorable year during which we held two of our greatest art exhibitions. One was a show of fifty-one oils and watercolours by James W. Morrice in April, and, in December, David Milne's first exhibition in Canada, of sixty canvases from some of his prime and most productive painting years. During that same twelve-month period we also had an extraordinary exhibition of paintings and drawings by Canada's artist-historian, Charles W. Jefferys. Incredible as it may seem now, our total gross sales from these three exhibitions amounted to less than $10,000, not enough, for example, to buy even a sketch by Morrice today.

At this time there was plenty of excellent art material to be found in Canada. Besides a show by Horatio Walker, we held a Homer Watson memorial exhibition in November 1936 through the auspices of the Waterloo Trust Company who administered the estate of the recently deceased artist. Its general manager, Philip V. Wilson, was a man of compassion who also sensed the artist's rightful place in Canadian art history. The company, in what at the time was a rare gesture of corporate generosity, provided Watson with enough money to live on during his declining years when he was unable to paint at all. There was otherwise no sale for his pictures. The foreword for the catalogue was written by Watson's good friend and colleague, the former president of the Royal Canadian Academy, Sir E. Wyly Grier, who extolled Watson's former status as "the outstanding figure in Canadian landscape art." The tragedy of all this was that by 1936 Watson's name was all but forgotten, and it would take the passing of another twenty-five years after his death before his art came back into favour. Another old friend of Watson's, Curtis Williamson, bewailed Watson's misfortune with the pronouncement that "He tried to go modern," meaning he had turned his back on the traditional painting practices that had served him so well in his earlier years. It was shortly after 1900, that Watson began to change his painting technique, loading his brush and building up a heavy impasto that produced a thick, rough porous-like surface on the canvas. The public recognized the pictures as artistic failures and turned its back on them.

There were fifty-four paintings in our Watson show with prices starting at a paltry $75. They included a few works prior to 1900, but mostly they were examples of his later style. We sold one, a 22" x 30" canvas, *Winter Moonrise*, to the Toronto industrialist, J. Ardah Scythes and even he insisted on a special price, or else he wouldn't buy it. He finally paid us $500 instead of the catalogue price of $750. Hard bargainer though Mr. Scythes was, I respected him and we later became good friends.

In the early 1930s there were no modern facilities where an artist could hold a one-man show. Our new establishment was chic and attractive, with good lighting and a private showing room. The gallery was therefore favourably regarded by artists anxious to hold exhibitions. We had many requests for two-week exhibition slots. Sometimes an artist approached us with an offer to rent the premises and still allow us a commission on sales. This was an offer not to be treated lightly because money was scarce for artists and dealers alike, and collecting a rental fee of $100 per week represented a significant sum. My own salary was $100 a month which was then sufficient to allow me to get married.

One such rental arrangement was an exhibition by Mrs. Mary Dignam, whose husband was a prosperous coal and wood merchant in Toronto. Mrs. Dignam also had shows in New York at the distinguished Knoedler Gallery on a rental basis. Like Claude Monet, Mary Dignam enjoyed painting water lily ponds, and was successful in capturing the essence of these perky white flowers floating among the opulent lily pads. A forceful, upright and strong-willed woman, prominent among women's art organizations, she can easily be looked on today as one of Canada's early feminists. Also she taught art to the young ladies at Moulton College. Born in 1860, Mrs. Dignam remained active in her painting activities until the late 1930s. Another of our early exhibitors, who also rented gallery space, was Jean Munro. I remember her as a person whose landscapes in soft autumnal colours were as warm and gentle as the lady herself. The work of both these artists enjoys a quiet respect today.

We showed the work of other women artists, such as the flower paintings of Clara Hagarty and watercolours by Geraldine

Wright, a Rosedale matron, wife of a judge. There were also the Brittons, Harry and his wife Henrietta. Harry was the more accomplished artist. However, since we had his pictures on a consignment basis it was easy to keep Henrietta happy by choosing a few of hers too. They lived in the Annex not far from our galleries. Harry Britton was an old-fashioned Edwardian gentleman, who was just as English as his name implied. He spent some years in Nova Scotia and painted many Canadian maritime themes.

One of our modest buyers in the mid-1930s was the Canadian chocolate king, Frank P. O'Connor, a poor country boy born near Peterborough. In 1913, he founded the phenomenally successful candy business, imaginatively named after Laura Secord, and featuring as a trademark a reproduction of Canada's appealing young War of 1812 heroine. Another reason for the company's outstanding success was the freshness of the product and the spotlessly clean white and black painted stores in which Mr. O'Connor offered sweets straight from his immaculate factory studios. I remember well his cherubic countenance, which belied his astute business sense. He was a great friend at the time of Ontario's mercurial premier, Mitchell Hepburn.

We exhibited a collection of paintings by Carl Ahrens in 1938. They came from the family of the gallant General Malcolm Mercer, who had bought a number of them to help the destitute artist survive. The pictures were studies of trees and forest interiors. Even though the notorious Hector Charlesworth, vociferous critic of the Group of Seven, wrote a glowing account of Ahrens and his work for our catalogue, the pictures were so dark and unattractive that we sold only one and that to our ever gracious patron, Mrs. George Gough.

It is not just the artists who make creative contributions to a community, in this case the town of Sarnia, but other people as well. Two individuals who highlighted the art scene of their day were the Torontonian , Dr. James M. MacCallum, and Miss Frances Flintoft, the latter being the leading figure of a little art group mainly responsible for bringing three Tom Thomson canvases to Sarnia in 1922.

One was *Chill November*, depicting a great flock of wild geese flying high through stormy northern skies. The artist, no doubt alerted by their honking, had felicitously sketched their fluid

48   Lawren Harris   *The Ramparts, B.C.*   c.1924

flight patterns. This painting was later formally presented to the Sarnia Public Library. At the same time, John Cowan, a Sarnia lawyer, purchased the canvas, *Morning Cloud*, a dramatic study of light and weather effects. The third painting, *Byng Island, Georgian Bay*, a landscape of windswept island pines was bought by R.V. Lesueur, an executive with the Imperial Oil Company in Sarnia, later its president. These acquisitions were arranged by the enthusiastic Miss Flintoft through Dr. MacCallum, Tom Thomson's friend and original patron. In 1937 we borrowed *Byng Inlet, Georgian Bay*, and the *Morning Cloud* canvases for our Tom Thomson loan exhibition celebrating the artist's birth in 1877, sixty years earlier.

After Tom Thomson's strange and unexplained demise at Canoe Lake in July 1917, Dr. MacCallum accepted the role of unofficial agent handling some of the pictures for sale on behalf of the estate. The doctor reacted strongly to the naturalism and mood of Thomson's paintings which reflected his own character and love of the northland. Perhaps this explains why he felt he understood the Thomson psyche better than anyone else. Dr. MacCallum also had definite ideas about the intrinsic value of the paintings and felt a deep responsibility for placing the few remaining canvases in the hands of those who truly appreciated their significance. By 1918, at least two important canvases and a number of sketches were sold through the doctor to the National Gallery of Canada.

In the mid-twenties the successful lumber dealer brothers Walter C. and Robert A. Laidlaw bought between them from the Thomson estate, forty or more sketches, through the offices of Lawren Harris and Dr. MacCallum at an average price of $50 each. It is strange that at the time they bought the sketches they didn't acquire a single canvas because there were some excellent ones still available. By 1926, the remaining canvases, some of which the doctor did not consider to be of the highest quality, were turned over to Tom's eldest brother, George, the titular head of the Thomson family. George Thomson then proceeded to store the canvases and sketches in the attic of his Owen Sound home until he released some of them to us for our great Tom Thomson exhibition of March 1937.

In the autumn of 1938, the Sarnia Art Association invited me to give a talk on Canadian art at the public library, and to exhibit some of our pictures, and it was there that I recall seeing Tom

Thomson's *Chill November* for the first time. For years the picture had been sequestered away, like many other Canadian paintings in semi-public collections such as Provincial Normal Schools, and in this case, a public library. I was therefore not surprised when I saw how dark and dirty it appeared. Instead of showing the vibrant colours the artist had used when he painted it, the picture was now dull and grey.

I made some good friends in Sarnia during that trip. One was Norman Gurd, a local lawyer, who after my talk insisted on taking me home for a "pot-luck" supper. There was also D. Park Jamieson, an early buyer of Group of Seven sketches, and active in various artistic pursuits. Also from Sarnia, and interested in the arts, was Pauline Mills McGibbon, a fellow student at Victoria College, who went on to become the first woman Lieutenant-Governor for the Province of Ontario. Another person who purchased pictures from us was H.M. Hueston, the publisher of the Sarnia newspaper.

Strange and unlikely anecdotes surface from time to time in the art world, and the following is certainly one of them. The disappearance in 1919 of Ambrose J. Small, the millionaire theatrical entrepreneur, was a case that was never solved. It remains one of Canada's most baffling and intriguing mysteries. Shortly after Mr. Small vanished into thin air, Theresa, his wife, or perhaps by then his widow, became a recluse.

For some years gossip had it that Ambrose Small had acquired a large number of fine Old Master paintings, but we knew no one who had actually seen the collection and could give us a valid report on their quality. Then abruptly, in 1936, some seventeen years after Mr. Small had disappeared, the entire collection of fifty-odd Old Master paintings was delivered to our Yonge Street galleries and we temporarily stored them. This was done by order of Mrs. Small's executors since the lady herself had recently died.

Full of anticipation, and in high hopes of finding some hidden masterpieces, a dream not impossible under the circumstances, we could hardly wait for an opportunity to examine them. That moment soon arrived and we began to study each picture in the strong daylight. Once I thought I saw a Salisbury Cathedral subject by Constable, but no such luck. From the corner of my eye I spied a marine subject with strong sunset colours that suggested Turner; again it was nothing but a school copy. Our expectations grew less and less as we continued to look at the pictures, until finally our hopes were completely dashed. The entire collection consisted of nothing but copies and fakes and had no value whatever. Thus another facet in the brazen character of the notorious Ambrose J. Small was revealed. Not only had he disappeared but he had gathered together what was probably the greatest collection of art-trash ever found in Canada.

Perhaps Mr. Small thought that his good eye for theatre was also a good eye for art, but if that was the way he perceived it, he was dead wrong. Small had travelled widely and certainly had the means to buy good pictures from reliable firms in London or New York. Whatever was it then that prompted him to buy all this rubbish? My guess is that he was mercilessly conned by roving dealers who happily sold him fake after fake and copy after copy.

Once, in the 1930s, Toronto art dealer A. Luscombe Carroll found in London a version, or replica, of *After the Bath* by Paul Peel, which he handed over to us for sale. Like his friend, Robert Mellors, my father's short-time partner in the early days of the business, Carroll had been trained in the art business in England and had no interest whatever in Canadian art. This Paul Peel discovery, however, turned into an important financial coup for Carroll.

After we placed the painting on view there was considerable newspaper interest, as it was regarded as a significant art find. Then controversy broke out regarding the picture's authenticity. Fortunately at the time, there still were two Paul Peel contemporaries living in Toronto who not only knew his work but had also known Peel as art students in Paris. One was the venerable academy painter George A. Reid, and the other the affable portrait artist Sir Wyly Grier. Both of these Paul Peel experts examined the painting carefully with much interest and each pronounced it a genuine work. There was a full-page spread about the Paul Peel discovery in the press.

Shortly afterwards we sold it to a young man who had recently inherited a large fortune. His name was C. Powell Bell, and he paid $10,000 for it, which was an astronomically high price for a picture by a Canadian artist at that time. (By comparison we had

49   André Lapine   *Captain Millar's Cottage, Lake Simcoe*   1933

116

good A.Y. Jackson canvases on consignment from the artist at prices from $300 to $600 and sketches at $35 apiece.) After nominal costs Carroll received nearly $5,000 as proceeds for his propitious discovery. It couldn't have come at a better time for him. Unfortunately Powell Bell died at an early age, and since then I have never been able to trace the whereabouts of the picture.

Many years later, in 1963, I purchased, among a significant group of Paul Peel paintings, a third version of *After the Bath* from the California resident, Mary Peel Hammond, a granddaughter of the artist. Mary Peel had also owned the original small study for the picture. Unfortunately the panel on which it was painted was marred by a split in the wood. This defect was not serious enough to ruin its quality and the attention of a good restorer was all that was needed to put it right, but I still remained somewhat diffident about including it with the others I was buying. In the end, Mary Peel decided to keep it as a memento. I recently learned that the little picture had been sold to the Art Gallery of Ontario. So, there exist today three large versions of *After the Bath* on canvas plus the small sketch panel and each is an original work by the hand of Paul Peel.

Throughout my story I have indicated that the public was apathetic towards Canadian art in the thirties. There were few coloured reproductions of Canadian art large enough to hang in school classrooms, for example, or any textbooks available containing information about the painters of Canada for schools and libraries. The few Canadian art books that then appeared in print were in small editions and even those took a long time to sell, if they sold at all. I remember in 1938 buying ten copies of Marius Barbeau's engaging book on Cornelius Krieghoff at Morgan's store in Montreal remaindered at 89¢ a copy. Today, of course, it's a valuable collector's item.

In New York in 1935, I saw striking colour reproductions of the French Impressionist and Post-Impressionist artists produced in Germany by the Munich firm of Hanfstangl and Company. Two years later my father and I decided it might be a good idea to have an important Canadian painting reproduced by the collotype process the Hanfstangl people had perfected. We selected J.E.H. MacDonald's *Tangled Garden*, probably the most controversial work painted by any member of the Group of Seven. Early in 1938 we shipped the large picture painted on heavy beaverboard to Germany, an innovative as well as expensive undertaking at the time. The final result was a magnificent colour print approximately 25″ x 30″ in size, in an edition of 500 copies.

This was the first large reproduction ever made of a Canadian painting by the German collotype process. We expected to sell it framed to schools for $24.50 and still make a profit. I crisscrossed hundreds of miles throughout Ontario, visiting schools and meeting with principals and art teachers (most of whom had never even heard of J.E.H. MacDonald) trying to convince them that the reproduction was a desirable addition to a classroom. Sometimes they would allow me to leave the picture on approval, but invariably on my return to Toronto from a two- or three-day trip, the pictures had preceded me, usually arriving with the carriage charges to be collected.

Strangely, the print was disparaged almost as much in 1938 as the original painting had been by certain art critics when first exhibited in 1916. It turned out that the choice of *The Tangled Garden* was a big mistake from a selling point of view. The closed-in overgrown garden somehow put people off. Certainly had we chosen one of MacDonald's Algoma landscapes with a stream tumbling over rapids and a distant view of the hills of the Pre-Cambrian Shield, in the artist's classic autumn colours, it probably would have been a much better seller. After the war, in 1947, and some hard bargaining with H.O. McCurry, we finally disposed of the two hundred or so remaining copies to the National Gallery at 50¢ each. Today this reproduction is a rare item, and seldom seen on the market.

In many ways Harry O. McCurry, Director of the National Gallery from 1939 to 1955, was the consummate civil servant, who happened to possess an excellent eye for a picture but unduly agonized in making a decision either to buy or not to buy. In the late 1930s we shipped off a collection of our choicest sketches by J.E.H. MacDonald for McCurry's attention and consideration by the gallery. Among them was the Algoma sketch, *October Shower Gleam* a richly coloured panel painted on one of MacDonald's usual 8 ½″ x 10 ½″ book-binding boards. McCurry recognized instantly the great quality of the sketch and after a long period of uncertainty finally bought it himself for $40. Of course it was a little masterpiece. The picture remained in the McCurry family until 1980, when we bought it at a public sale in Toronto for $82,500.

119

Frederick S. Coburn working in Montreal and Franz Johnston in Toronto were undoubtedly the two most popular Canadian artists of the 1930s. During the years from 1937 to 1951, I used to visit Coburn at his grey stone-fronted studio home on Crescent Avenue near the Ritz Carlton Hotel in Montreal. By 1937, he was in his mid-sixties and still painting his typical winter landscapes with horses and sleighs in Eastern Township settings. Coburn seldom had anything on hand in his studio for sale. It took time to learn how to do business with Fred Coburn, but once his confidence was gained, he was very easy to deal with. Our usual method was to commission pictures in the $400-to-$600 price range depending on the size and subject. For example, a canvas with two sleighs and horses, even though the same size, would cost slightly more than a canvas with a single sleigh and horse. Depending on how busy he was, it usually took him two to three weeks to complete a commission.

Just a five-minute walk from Coburn's studio was the Watson Art Gallery. For many years William Watson had working for him a person by the name of Benny Grant. Benny was a most competent employee who could turn his hand cheerfully to almost any kind of job. He was useful as a salesman and could regale customers with amusing stories about artists. One of Benny's special missions was to call on Coburn from time to time. The artist liked him and so Benny often returned home with a canvas under his arm.

Frederick Coburn was a short, slight man, lively and fun-loving. Long a widower, he lived alone, but he liked the company of young ladies and every Saturday night went ballroom dancing well into the wee small hours of the morning. This was one of his ways of enjoying life and he did in fact consider himself quite professional on the dance floor. It must have been something to watch the old chap trip the light fantastic with the girls. During my many trips to his studio over the years I recall that he talked more about his dancing prowess than about art. However, Frederick Coburn was a good draughtsman and colourist, well-schooled in Europe, who in his earlier days painted fine still lifes, nudes, and interior studies.

In the years following the First World War he developed the style and subject matter that would make him famous: Quebec snowscapes with horses or oxen pulling sleighs. Picture buyers loved these paintings mainly because they were nostalgic, evoking memories of youthful visits to rural Quebec. Coburn was therefore more

50   Horatio Walker   *Hauling Firewood, Isle of Orleans*   1912

or less trapped into spending the rest of his painting life producing his popular sleigh scenes, the only subject the public was interested in buying. Had he moved into other subjects, it would have resulted in a considerable loss of income, pride, and prestige. I believe I bought my last painting from Fred Coburn in 1951.

I often used to see the artist John Russell, who had a large studio at the corner of Yonge and College Streets where he also conducted an art school. John Russell had lived and studied for years in Paris and had painted a series of attractive scenes of children playing with hoops and sailing boats in the fountains of Paris parks and public gardens. When he returned to Canada in 1932 he was briefly in high fashion as a portrait painter and became a familiar figure in midtown Toronto. Continuing to dress like a Parisian *boulevardier*, he sported a cane and wore the inevitable grey spats, but by this time his once elegant attire was becoming well worn and a little archaic. On certain occasions after a few drinks, he had been known to appear at a picture auction sale, stand up at a tense moment of action and loudly denounce the lot in hand as a fake, much to the great embarrassment of the auctioneer. But abrasive and non-conformist as he was, he passionately believed in his own judgement. I found him an honest and sincere man.

It was the fees from his art school that kept John Russell's body and soul together during the 1930s. In 1934 he conceived an idea he was sure would generate publicity and help sell pictures. The plan was to show a large collection of paintings, including female nudes many of which he had painted during his long sojourn in France, in rented space in one of the Canadian National Exhibition buildings during the period of the fair. Although this event took place during one of the most dismal years of the Depression, the press brought the show considerable notoriety, thoroughly titillating the sleepy old Toronto public. Despite warnings and threats from the "powers that be" to close the show down the exhibition continued to attract many visitors and ended up by making a decent profit.

In a personal foreword to his catalogue, Mr. Russell took note of his own special virtues as a painter, confidently ranking himself with Paul Peel, Blair Bruce, and James W. Morrice, as the great artists of the North American continent. But John Russell was becoming more and more cynical and gloomy. In 1935, he wrote for his catalogue, "I honestly cannot see any future for art on this Continent. . . . The economic pressure is perhaps too hard for the average artist and student to combat today. The world is becoming more materialistic every day and has always denied real genius its true place." I wonder what John Russell would have thought of the world of 1982.

Franklin Arbuckle was still in his twenties when he first showed with us in 1938. His wife, Frances Anne Johnston was also an artist of ability and the daughter of the famous Franz, a founding member of the Group of Seven. Young Arbuckle possessed great natural talent and I remember vividly the paintings in that show, landscapes, studies of horses, and rural subjects executed in the rich palette of an accomplished colourist. Business was so bad that in the early 1940s Franklin Arbuckle moved to Montreal and devoted most of his time to commercial art. By the 1950s, in my opinion, he was probably Canada's best commercial artist, completing a series of fascinating paintings for the cover of *Maclean's* Magazine. Fortunately he continued to paint his superb outdoor sketches and when I called on him during the 1950s at his Montreal studio he usually let me have some attractive panels or maybe even a canvas to take home.

It was about 1939 that we first began to handle the work of Frederick H. Brigden. As early as 1907, more than ten years before Lawren Harris's and A.Y. Jackson's first visits there, he was sketching along the north shore of Lake Superior at Rossport and Michipicoten. He once told me about getting lost deep in the Lake Superior bush country and for two days wondering if he would ever get out alive. As a young man he was an intrepid and adventurous artist and painted in Canada from Cape Breton Island to the shores of the Pacific.

A cheerful man of great integrity and character, Fred Brigden lived in the hamlet of Newtonbrook, about fifteen miles northeast of Toronto, in a simple farm cottage overlooking the valley of the Don River. Here he painted many of his fluent watercolours and oil sketches. About once a month, usually on a Monday morning, he would bring in one or two of his pastoral landscapes to leave with us for sale, and in late October, during the nutting season he would arrive with baskets of piquant black walnuts harvested from the grove at the rear of his small farm holdings.

When Fred Brigden died in 1955, the executors requested that we gather together all his oil sketches, watercolours, and canvases, and temporarily store them in the gallery. Brigden left his entire collection to the Y.M.C.A., an institution with which he had a life-long connection, but stipulated that any piece considered of poor or indifferent quality should be destroyed. We were assigned the task of sorting out the material and deciding which pieces should be consigned to the fire and which should be kept for sale. This rather tricky and responsible decision was carried out by my father and myself. We proceeded to weed out some 500 pieces, many half-finished works which we felt sure the artist would never have wanted to place on the market. These were then tossed into a bonfire in our backyard. All the remaining pictures were turned over to the Y.M.C.A. and later offered to the public at bargain-basement prices. A Bloor Street neighbour came round to the rear of his building to see what was going on with all the fire and smoke. He watched incredulously for a moment or two as the fire blazed away. "You're not going to burn up all those good paintings, are you?" he queried, in a state of complete shock. "Let me have them," he pleaded. My father responded that we were simply carrying out the late artist's wishes. Our neighbour continued to contemplate the blaze with extreme apprehension but finally acknowledged my father's determination to finish the job. Looking back on that occasion now, I find our neighbour's desire to recover some of those pictures for himself quite a natural and normal response. I even wonder myself how I would feel today about making another similar bonfire.

For thirty-four years we were Manly MacDonald's exclusive dealer and apart from personally selling some of his own work he refused to show his pictures with any other dealer or agent. It was an informal arrangement built solidly on trust and friendly association. Born at Port Anne in 1889, Manly had a great love of rural Ontario; the old mills, farm buildings, and work horses in the bush. These were the recurring themes of his outdoor compositions. He was adept at catching the effects of light on rivers or streams during spring breakups.

When in the city Manly MacDonald lived in south Rosedale in a Victorian house tucked snugly up on a small hill approached by a long flight of steps. He drove a dilapidated car in which he was always on the move to a favourite painting location, often returning

51   Albert Robinson   *Malbaie, Quebec*   1927

home with medium- and large-size canvases almost completed except for some finishing touches and a signature, to be added later in his studio. Many a time we talked about having a one-man exhibition and although sales were fairly steady, we all had serious reservations that any such show could prove a success. A man dedicated and devoted to his art, Manly MacDonald had little interest in money and never compromised himself by painting pictures purely to sell. His canvases, large and small, were always done out of doors on the spot. He stoically endured the bitterest of winter weather and would happily risk frostbite on his small exposed nose in order to finish a canvas before the uncertain winter afternoon light had gone. Every week or so he would bring to the galleries two or three finished paintings. He was a wonderfully optimistic soul who firmly believed his new paintings were always an improvement because he had discovered a new painting place. Of course that was not so but if Manly believed it everyone else was happy.

MacDonald was one of J.W. Beatty's former students who completely broke away from his teacher's influence and happily found his own unique painting style. He always had fresh plans for sketching trips and loved maple-sugar bush scenes, the farmers busy with horses loading wagons with barrels of sap. Every spring as a gift he would bring a gallon or two of fresh maple syrup from one of these harvests.

Manly MacDonald felt hurt that he did not receive the just appreciation he believed he deserved from fellow artists like Arthur Lismer and especially A.Y. Jackson, who himself basked in such sunny acclaim.

I am truly sorry that he never lived to see the day when he would be recognized as one of Canada's excellent artists. That fruition would not come until some ten years after his death.

I first met Sam Borenstein in 1939 when he had come to Toronto from Montreal with a portfolio of canvases to sell. Born in Lithuania, he had emigrated to Canada as a boy with members of his family. A man of nervous intensity he was happy to get rid of his paintings for $20 each. At this time all I could do was help him sell a few pictures to my friends. My Amsterdam partner Peter Eilers, for example, bought one of his canvases, which still hangs in his home at Laren, Holland. Later Borenstein became a private picture dealer operating from his home in Montreal and did much better financially. I remember an outsize Jackson painting featuring an orang-ish rock pile which hung over Jackson's mantelpiece in the Studio Building. It was important in size but at the time something I could never have sold. Borenstein, however, bought it in 1955, just before Jackson moved from Toronto to Manotick, and soon had it resold.

Unfortunately Sam didn't live to see the day when his own pictures would be selling for large sums and a book would be published on his work. One of the difficulties was that he was generally considered a derivative artist highly influenced by the art of van Gogh and Soutine.

During the thirties, Perkins Bull, one of Toronto's most colourful figures, was engaged in writing a twelve-volume historical series on Toronto and Peel County and while doing so commissioned many drawings by Charles W. Jefferys. In 1934, we gave C.W. Jefferys the first exhibition he ever held with a private dealer. Jefferys knowledge of Canada's history, gained by lifetime study, was immense, and though his drawings sometimes suffered from a certain stiffness in execution he nevertheless recreated events of history and made them come alive. I did not realize then the remarkable qualities of this artist-historian, but his work was, I believe, superior to that of any other Canadian artist who attempted similar themes. I don't think we sold a single picture from that exhibition.

Jefferys was a slight, short man with a white moustache. He chainsmoked cigarettes and one side of his otherwise pristine white moustache was permanently stained brown. Disappointed at the lack of sales, but nevertheless cheerful, he maintained an optimistic outlook on life. Some years after Charles W. Jefferys died, in 1952, one of the big international oil companies bought up the contents of his studio. Of course now the Charles W. Jefferys name has become justly famous.

A White Russian *emigré* who had studied in Europe before settling in western Canada, Nickola de Grandmaison was another artistic and eccentric individualist. He was very ambitious and nothing was too much trouble to help make a sale or win a portrait commission. He was a master of the pastel medium. Grandmaison approached us in 1937 with the suggestion that we be his exclusive agents in Toronto. He brought in a large portfolio of pastels featuring Blackfoot Indian chiefs as well as a series of dark-eyed appealing papooses. These pastels were drawn on large sheets of exquisitely fine sandpaper with a light tan background. Besides providing a satisfactory surface, the sandpaper locked in the pastel pigment, eliminating much of the danger of smudging. We were successful in arranging several commissions for Grandmaison and also sold a number of pastels. But Nick, as we called him, was too temperamental and restless a person to carry out even a short-term contract with a commercial gallery.

Another western artist whose work we acquired was Walter J. Phillips. He sent us watercolours and portfolios of his attractive and colourful rice paper wood blocks. He was a fine print maker and each piece was signed by the artist and offered to the public at $5 and $10 apiece. Despite the low prices, there was little interest in prints at the time.

We also showed the work of the dentist painter, Dr. Gordon Pearson, as well as that of George Broomfield, Lionel Thomas, Caven Atkins, and Ernest Dalton, the furrier and Olympic fencing competitor. In addition, there were artists like Richard Choate, the journalist, James Henderson from the Qu'Appelle Valley, André Lapine, John Clymer, Winnifred Needler, and many others. There were the watercolours of undulating grain fields and abandoned farm houses by the Hanover, Ontario-born Carl Schaefer. Today, highly respected, Schaefer's work was original and personal but almost completely ignored in the thirties.

Portraiture was a world onto its own but there were still a few important portrait commissions available in the thirties. Such plums as commissions to paint retiring bank presidents and heads of large business institutions, or high court judges, and occasionally at a lower fee a high school principal, perhaps about to be superannuated. There was great competition for these commission plums. Among the portrait artists trying to make ends meet at the time were Kenneth Forbes, Archibald Barnes, Allan Barr, and Sir E. Wyly Grier, the final name a knight among the dwindling survivors of the art of classical portraiture. We knew them all as they were regular visitors to our gallery.

Wyly Grier was knighted in 1935, by George V, in recognition of his achievements as a portrait painter. What a striking show twenty-five or so of Grier's best portraits, painted between 1900 and 1930, would make today. It would be a veritable microcosm of the

52   J.E.H. MacDonald   *Cliffs Near Hubert, Montreal River, Algoma*   1919

period and would include the names of many of our great and near great Canadians like the financier art connoisseur Sir Edmund Walker, John W. Dafoe, the legendary *Winnipeg Free Press* editor, Sir Oliver Mowat, W. Perkins Bull, et al.

Others, such as Charles MacGregor, possessed amazing resilience to have survived at all as portrait painters in that era. We got MacGregor a commission or two but what really saved him was that he was able to escape to the Maritimes to paint a lieutenant-governor or some other dignitary there. It was not just by mere chance that nearly all his patrons in the Maritime Provinces also had Scottish names.

As difficult as times were in the thirties, they were for me also challenging years of great learning. The foundation of our business gradually built up in those times would slowly begin to bear fruit in the decade following. The only thing that kept us going at all was the fact that there was usually someone just coming in from the wings who, on seeing a picture that caught their fancy, would move heaven and earth just to find the money to buy it. Such a person was A.S. "Shy" Mathers, the distinguished architect known for his well-designed neo-Georgian houses. In 1937 he bought a large 1930 Lawren Harris canvas for $400, when Harris was known only to the *cognoscenti*. Sherlock Mathers bought many oustanding pictures from us over the years. Fortunately there were a few others of the same mould as "Shy" Mathers. Most of these people had little spare cash, but their hearts smouldered with a burning desire to own certain works of art which they had first seen in our galleries; certainly they were acquisitive people but in the very best sense of the word. The wonderful thing was that they bought the pictures simply because they loved them, never dreaming that some day in the future their children or grandchildren might be able to resell them at a huge profit. Throughout those years we were thankful for the patronage of the individuals who comprised our little band of compulsive and joyful art collectors.

What Claude Pascoe's background was I do not know exactly and he rarely talked about his business or profession. Actually he was a personal assistant to Joseph E. Atkinson, the recalcitrant newspaper genius, and politically powerful publisher of the *Toronto Star*. Pascoe was a skilled troubleshooter on behalf of "Holy Joe," as he was sometimes irreverently referred to on the pages of certain competing newspapers. He was a big man with a round face and a disarmingly affable countenance, who, according to gossip, could be completely ruthless in the course of his duties. Claude Pascoe would sometimes sit down to study a picture completely oblivious to the fact that a cigarette was burning in his mouth, and the ashes would fall onto his waistcoat. Invariably he was accompanied by his little red-haired wife, the top of whose head barely reached his shoulders.

Pascoe was a dedicated amateur artist and one of his great pleasures in life was the privilege of copying flower paintings by his favourite French artist Henri Fantin Latour. Sometimes we had examples of Fantin's work for sale and Pascoe would ask if he could take the painting home for a weekend in order to copy it. This was a request we found difficult to refuse. Later he would proudly produce his copy to show us how clever an artist he was. We soon realized that the best way to handle the problem was to keep any flower paintings by Fantin Latour completely out of sight.

One of the most singular of our clients was Samuel E. Weir, who practised law in London, Ontario. He was a big lumbering figure of a man, who wore out-of-fashion clothes that were invariably rumpled. He had a round face and a mouth that spread from ear to ear when he laughed. He was a good story teller with a bawdy twist to his humour. His personality would come alive when relating some of the happenings and incidents during his travels, particularly about artists he knew in Canada and England. He possessed a sharp mind, and was another of those individualists I have been talking about. Sam relished the role. An aggressive trial lawyer, he combined an international practice with a local one, maintaining an apartment-office in New York where he travelled regularly on business.

I got to know Sam Weir in the late 1930s, during my formative years in the picture business. He continued to visit us and buy the odd picture until late in the sixties. Travelling to Toronto frequently on legal business he always stayed at the Albany Club in downtown Toronto. A Methodist parson's son he could be irascible and difficult at times, but I also knew him as one of those rare individuals completely without prejudice towards his fellow man. In today's sense he was a populist and the idea of discriminating against someone because of station in life, ethnic or religious background, would never have occurred to him. When time permitted from his law practice he haunted the premises of dealers in old books, manuscripts, and maps.

Sam would help anyone in trouble, in his legal capacity, particularly artists and others who existed on the fringes of the art world, like the Wenwraths and Pritzkers, the second-hand booksellers, and the picture restorer, Frank Worrall, whose sometimes fanciful opinions on pictures Sam always accepted as gospel truth. I remember about 1938, when Saul Wenwrath discovered two marvellous portraits of Indian chiefs by Paul Kane. Unfortunately Sam Weir missed out on them, but they were so desirable that they soon ended up in the permanent collection of the Montreal Art Association.

Some years later Sam Weir discovered the geographical beauty and ideal climate of the little Central American Republic, Costa Rica. He established a home there where he retreated from the hard Canadian winters for a few weeks each year. He often talked about beautiful Costa Rica and he tried hard to learn Spanish. Long unmarried, he was quite taken with the physical charms of the women there. Later, when his twin sister died, Sam, the confirmed old bachelor, met and fell in love with a young and beautiful Costa Rican girl and married her. He brought his bride, Rosa Maria, home to Queenston, where by then, having ceased practising law, he was spending nearly all his waking hours working on his Canadiana collection. On several occasions he invited me to visit him and see the place, which he hoped one day would be open to the public.

One day in early September 1976 I was in nearby Thorold, engaged in buying back some paintings we had years ago sold to an old collector and friend, Katherine Bean. After concluding my business with Miss Bean I decided to telephone Sam Weir. When the phone rang, I heard a voice answer, then complete silence followed. I dialled again and got a busy signal. I then realized Sam must have left the phone off the hook to discourage further calls. It was a magnificent warm autumn day and since I was so close to Queenston at the time, I decided to chance a visit. I soon arrived at his fine new house, built in colonial style and recently completed, which he'd aptly named "Riverview," since it was situated on the high cliffs overlooking the awesome Niagara gorge. I parked the car and

53 Frederick H. Brigden *Valley on the Don River* c.1940

walked up the short driveway. There I encountered a barrage of intimidating signs such as "No trespassing," "Beware of concealed traps," "Visitors are not welcome," and others even more menacing. This was typical of Sam's way of overreacting to a situation he found difficult to cope with, namely discouraging casual visitors from dropping in unannounced. However, Sam made me feel at home and proceeded to slowly escort me throughout the establishment, all the while doing the talking.

The house was in a state of terrible confusion. Art books, old issues of art journals by the hundreds, and manuscripts were strewn about waiting to be catalogued, he said. He showed me two Tom Thomson sketches with their frames screwed flat against the wall. One was the magnificent original sketch for the *Jack Pine*, perhaps Canada's most famous painting. Sam Weir had actually picked up the two Tom Thomsons some thirty years earlier in the T. Eaton Company's picture department. The story was that the artist had sold the pictures to American summer visitors at Algonquin Park in 1916. Years later in 1946, they turned up for sale at Eaton's. Sam proceeded to buy them over the telephone for $300 each. Then there was superb Lawren Harris sketch and a good landscape by Homer Watson, also two lovely small panels by J.W. Morris and an important Cornelius Krieghoff autumn landscape as well as portraits and other Canadiana studies. Sam was a born collector with an urge to buy almost anything he liked and thought would somehow fit into his overall Canadiana collection.

Sam Weir suffered greatly from ill health during the last several years of his life, but he still managed to get around. Then out of the blue at the end of July 1980, six months before he died, at age eighty-two, I received a long and buoyant letter from him, congratulating me on my book and outlining his plans for the eventual use of his house, as a library-art gallery, open to the public.

I think he would have permitted himself a huge chuckle of satisfaction if he could have seen the stories about him in the newspapers following his death.

Sam wanted to go down in history remembered as the creator of the Weir Foundation and especially for his great devotion to the art and history of English-speaking Canada. The press reported in headlines, "Sam guards his treasures from his grave." No mention was made in the obituary (which he probably composed him-

54   Manly MacDonald   *Hauling Wood, Near Point Anne, Ontario*   c.1940

self) that he was ever married.

I am sure that many people will be eagerly looking forward to the opening of the gallery-library that Sam Weir created. His wish was granted that he be entombed within the grounds of his beloved house at Queenston – a special concession to one who had willed his estate to the people of Canada as a memorial museum.

7

Art Dealing During and
After World War II

We knew that we had to run a pretty tight ship if we hoped to survive another decade in the art business. So far it had been a long, hard struggle. Therefore, in 1941, to save expenses, we bought a handsome Victorian house on Bloor Street east where the Hudson's Bay centre now stands, and converted it into a gallery.

We had a reasonably good collection of European pictures on hand at the time including some works by the Impressionist and Barbizon Schools. These and others were consigned to us for sale by the art collector-publisher of the *Ottawa Citizen*, H.S. Southam. During the war years shipments from England were curtailed or cut off by the devastating German U-boat offensive in the North Atlantic, but fortunately we were able to obtain numerous pictures for sale from estates and trust companies. We also realized that the future success of the business depended on our getting more and more involved with contemporary Canadian artists. This we continued to do, and it would be quite fair to say that at one time or another we had connections with virtually every Canadian artist of consequence during that period. Some associations lasted thirty and more years, others were quite brief.

I still look back in amazement at the large number of ima-

137

ginative and even spectacular exhibitions we held in the thirties. While largely ignored by the public and commercially unsuccessful, they helped provide a rich and cumulative background that would strengthen our business in the future. Also they were great growing and learning years for me. Nineteen-thirty-nine marked the end of a decade that somehow seemed to depart reluctantly, and the beginning of another war that was supposed to end all wars but would last itself for more than five whole years.

The war also saw the coming of age of Canada as an industrial nation, and thousands of people from the country migrated to the cities of Quebec and Ontario to work in munitions and other war-related industries. In the thirties, Canada was still largely an agricultural economy. Indeed upwards of 75 per cent of our population was rurally oriented, living on farms and in small towns and villages. But the 1930s turned out to be the last decade of a predominantly rural Ontario and Quebec. Quite naturally artists were painting what they saw as bucolic scenes of Ontario and Quebec countryside, pastoral landscapes that were easy to look at but seldom innovative or extreme. The artists considered themselves fortunate if they could just sell enough pictures to live on. I concede that we did not consider them great artists at the time but rather a source of good painting at reasonable prices that we could sell as bread-and-butter pieces in the gallery. But times have changed, and today the works of many of these artists are considered an important part of the Canadian art heritage – and rightly so.

In September 1940, we decided to branch out a little more and hold an exhibition and sale of Canadian paintings in Hamilton, Ontario. Since there were no commercial galleries there at the time, we settled instead for space on the second floor of Cunningham's downtown photography store. The Art Gallery of Hamilton was then located in an old public building which was infrequently visited. Its collection consisted mainly of a group of large studio works by Blair Bruce bequeathed to Hamilton, the city of the artist's birth, by his Swedish widow Caroline. Today in faraway Sweden an even larger collection of his work exists at Brucebo, where the Blair Bruce Art Gallery is located on the Island of Gotland in the Baltic Sea.

For the Hamilton exhibition I borrowed six paintings of Algonquin Park and Port Hope from J.W. Beatty. The prices were

55 Franklin Carmichael *Autumn in the Northland* 1921

in the $400-to-$500 range. However, paintings by Beatty, or any other Canadian artist for that matter, aroused no interest at all among the few Hamilton citizens who were curious enough to view our show. In the end I left most of the pictures with Mr. Cunningham for an extra ten days, and then returned to Toronto.

Our most consistent buyer in Hamilton was the Hamilton Club, which set aside an annual budget for pictures and in a most daring purchase in 1945 bought the controversial canvas, *Birch Grove, Autumn* by Tom Thomson for $5,000. This acquisition caused an acrimonious debate among the club members. However, the picture committee, consisting of Lester Husband, a local architect, and Joseph Piggott, the well-known general contractor, let the storm blow over, and allowed the sale to remain final. The painting remained on the walls of the Hamilton Club for many years until it was purchased by Roy Cole, a club member, who graciously presented it to the Art Gallery of Hamilton as a memorial to his parents.

When T.R. MacDonald became curator of the Art Gallery of Hamilton in 1947, things began to change for the better and the gallery slowly took on a fresh new direction. Within a few years it moved into a new building near McMaster University. Although the institution was perpetually starved for funds, Tom MacDonald had a special talent for rooting out good pictures at bargain prices. He always seemed able to raise the money if he found some picture he considered special and badly wanted to acquire for the gallery. A significant part of the Hamilton gallery's permanent collection is certainly the result of Tom MacDonald's astute buying. Everyone respected the man for his sensitivity, good taste, and pleasing manners. He was also an artist in his own right, doing interiors and figure subjects. He had an innate appreciation of the work of other artists, tenacity, and the ability to unearth things of the best quality for his art museum. For a long time he was a man of uncertain health and during the last few years of his life suffered more and more from an overwhelming fatigue that seriously hampered his activities. His name should be remembered as the individual responsible for the building of the Art Gallery of Hamilton's collection to its present level of excellence. We reached our lowest ebb in sales during 1942, when our total gross income for the whole year sank to an abysmal $22,340, hardly enough to buy a half-decent Group of

Seven sketch today. With a war on, some people contended that the diversion of funds into art, even Canadian, was unpatriotic. They believed that the money should be used instead to buy Victory Bonds. However, after Montgomery's pivotal victory of November 1942, at El Alamein in the North African desert, the public breathed a collective sigh of relief, now confident that the Allies would win the war. Indeed after El Alamein, the stock markets began their long steady rise and even the picture business improved.

Around 1940 we began to contact Montreal artists whose work we thought might find favour in Toronto. One was Berthe des Clayes whom I called on at her Beaver Hall Square studio in Montreal. For years she had been painting Quebec winter scenes of horse and sleigh subjects that were quite popular. Miss des Clayes was a good craftswoman in both the oil and pastel mediums. A tiny woman, born in Scotland, she was quiet and shy, and had two sisters who also were painters. Approachable and agreeable she was delighted to lend us a number of her paintings to try and sell in Toronto – our commission being the usual one-third of the selling price.

Another Quebec artist, Paul Caron, had died in 1941, and early in the following year I visited his daughter Lorraine, who had inherited her father's estate. Unfortunately there were few oils as her father had sold most of them for a pittance during his lifetime. But this young woman, warm and attractive, seemed delighted to find anyone at all interested in buying or selling her father's work. As I recall there were only three or four oil paintings available, the estate consisting mainly of watercolours of habitant village subjects. In 1941, it was quite impossible to find a market for watercolours and I returned home with only a couple of small canvases. I left all the watercolours behind with Lorraine. I have often since thought about Paul Caron's daughter and wondered how she fared during the later years of her life.

Henri Masson, the Belgian-born Ottawa artist was a forthright man whose work was introduced to me by Harry S. Southam. Mr. Southam the perennial chairman of the board of trustees of the National Gallery of Canada, must have, in the late forties, bought nearly all of Masson's output. He then presented these works to universities (Queen's received at least thirteen of Masson's paintings) and various other institutions scattered around the country. Mr. Southam was one of a handful of connoisseur-patrons who

141

helped sustain the arts during these years.

From time to time, I visited Henri Masson at his modest Ottawa studio. It was there, in January 1947, that I bought my first group of pictures from him, and I particularly enjoyed a still life of ripe red strawberries lying on a table which hung in my home for several years. In those days when I was buying his paintings I thought of his work as decorative, colourful, and engaging. For instance he often enlivened his landscapes and street scenes with people and children. Today his one-man exhibitions are almost instant sellouts. Indeed Masson is regarded along with Casson and Biéler as one of Canada's grand old masters. Years ago he modestly admitted that I was the first dealer to buy his work outright. At present he has dealer outlets all over Canada and has no need of me.

There was another Montrealer, Thomas Garside, who painted winter scenes in the style of Maurice Cullen. He was a friend of the Montreal dealer Gerald Stevens (later the expert on early Canadian glass), who introduced me to his work. Garside was eventually appointed administrator of the Greenshields Foundation which provided funds for certain promising figurative or naturalistic artists. John Fox, whose work we showed in the mid-1950s, was among the recipients of a generous grant that allowed him to study in Italy.

Today, throughout Canada, a new generation of researchers and budding art historians are searching out unfamiliar and little-known artists. One of these is Fred N. Loveroff, a Russian-born, Saskatchewan artist who studied in Toronto under J.W. Beatty. We are also hearing something now of John Martin who, in 1949, painted a splendid study of Toronto's historic Cawthra mansion at King and Bay streets, before it was demolished to make way for the new Bank of Nova Scotia building.

These lesser-known artists include L.A.C. Panton, who was a tall solemn-faced man. He took his painting life seriously, was also a bit of a wit. He was an art teacher at the Northern Vocational School in Toronto and an excellent one. Later he became principal of the Ontario College of Art. We had several Panton exhibitions but always with little success. Much of his work was painted in dark earthy tones which had no appeal to the public.

Sidney Hallam, a friend of Panton's, was a full-time commercial artist. He also found time to paint enough to regularly exhi-

56   Clarence Gagnon   *Une rue de Baie St. Paul*   c.1923

bit in O.S.A. and Academy shows. He had good natural ability and would have become an even better artist had he been able to devote his full time to painting. We regularly showed and sold his work but he couldn't produce enough pictures to create a steady market. He died at a relatively early age in 1953.

William Winter enjoyed painting children and made hundreds of studies of them, indoors and out. Normally he worked on small panels and his pictures are wonderfully colourful. I feel Winter's lively little compositions have not received the recognition they deserve. For years he was a partner in the commercial art firm of Wookey, Bush and Winter. Jack Bush, the second partner, remained a commercial artist until he reached the age of nearly fifty. He then become involved in non-objective painting and through a combination of a New York critic's lavish praise, and good promotion and publicity, gained a name for himself as an important painter of "soft-edged" abstracts.

Among the painters whose works we had for sale in the 1940s, were Richard Jack, Stanley Royal, Herbert Palmer, Winchell Price, Tom Roberts, Frederick Haines, Harold McCrea, Yvonne Houser, York Wilson, Roland Gissing, Jack Shadbolt, and Leonard Brooks. Each of these artists has a niche within the total Canadian art spectrum.

In my mind an important artist was Robert Pilot. Born in 1898, in St. John's, Newfoundland, he was a stepson of the great landscape painter Maurice Cullen. Tutored early in life by his stepfather, Pilot later went on to a highly successful career of his own and achieved top status among artist organizations as well. As a young man, Pilot had travelled and studied in Europe, and on occasion had visited his father's Quebec sketching companion, James W. Morrice, in Paris. From the 1930s on he and his wife Patricia were active in the influential English-speaking high society of Westmount, in Montreal. This helped him develop a good market for his work and in no way interfered with his painting talents.

We had our first Pilot show in 1948, and continued for some years to acquire and exhibit his pictures. I still possess a letter

57 Tom Thomson *Pink Birches, Spring* c.1916

144

that expresses something of the urbanity and old-world courtesy of the man. He was writing about his paintings and begins, "My dear Blair," ending, "Your obedient servant, Robert Pilot." Archaic perhaps, but it tells something of the dignity of this man and the esteem in which he held us.

Robert Pilot was, at his best, one of Canada's finest artists. His early works of lower-town Quebec City and streetscapes of Montreal catch the piquant Gallic charm of these places and are a delight to look at – an aspect that anglophone artists often expressed better than their French counterparts. Later in his career, unfortunately, he lost some of his subtle colour sense and sometimes his compositions developed a strange off-the-axis tilt. This was no doubt caused by visual problems.

Pilot's friend Harold Beament, born the same year as Pilot, also lived in Montreal. He was among the earlier artists to make trips to the Arctic, painting the Inuit fishing from their kayaks, seal hunts on the ice floes, and other Arctic subjects. Harold and my father were good friends and the artist always came to Toronto for his exhibition openings. After five o'clock, the two would retreat to a comfortable spot in the gallery to conclude business for the day with a drink.

Among our patrons there were some memorable people who also became good friends. One was Stanford C. Dack, the president of Canada's finest shoe manufacturers, an old family business. Stan Dack had an active interest in Canadian art and bought many Canadian pictures from us. He was a dark-haired man with a short-cropped moustache. His manner was rather brusque but he had a heart of gold whenever struggling artists were concerned. As early as the mid-thirties he bought from Curtis Williamson, primarily to help out the artist.

He was also fond of fishing for small-mouthed bass. One weekend in July 1941 we decided to go to Tobermory, the little fishing village at the tip of the Bruce Peninsula, where we stayed overnight at a little hotel on which my father held a mortgage. Liquor was strictly rationed by the government during those war years and I bought a bottle of scotch to take with us for the trip. But unknown to me, Stan liked Canadian rye, and when I produced the scotch it was much to his disappointment and chagrin, as he abhorred the taste of scotch. The fish weren't biting either, but we

58 Maurice Cullen *Cutting Ice, Sillery Cove* c.1912

nevertheless enjoyed our day out on the waters of Georgian Bay. When he departed to California for good, he became yet another person whose friendship I greatly missed.

One of our interesting friends from those days was Dr. Arnold Mason, the dean of the Faculty of Dentistry. He was a warm and friendly man and a long-time patron of Canadian art. He was the type of person who not only agreed to sit for his own portrait by Frederick Varley, but arranged other commissions for the artist as well. He bought J.E.H. MacDonald paintings while the artist was still alive, and through us continued to acquire paintings by Curtis Williamson. I remember too Dr. Harold Box, the scientist-peridontist, and professor at the University of Toronto, who was an early buyer of J.W. Beatty paintings.

These are some of the people who bring back vivid memories; they are also among the first to show a practical interest and faith in Canadian art by buying work of these then totally unsung artists. The fact is that the art world is not just made up of the character and personality of the artists, but of those of the buyer as well.

My father always regarded Alfred J. Casson and Charles Comfort as two of the most important figures in the artist community, not necessarily the greatest painters but men who should be kept in touch with. Active in various art groups and societies they both rose to become their high officials. In those days Casson was still working as a full-time commercial artist at the Sampson-Matthews firm, and his painting activities were confined to holidays and weekends. However, somehow or other through the years, he managed to produce a volume of work equal to that of many artists who spent their whole life painting full time. His employer, an uncommon and durable man was C.A.G. Matthews, the company president. "I enjoyed working there," Casson said, "and besides I had a family to look after."

During the 1940s we showed paintings by Casson but even at minuscule prices they hardly ever sold. Our records indicate that as late as 1957, the most we received for one of his large works, a splendid canvas of 1926, was $750. In 1958, when he retired from Sampson-Matthews, after working there for thirty-two years, we were still offering his small panels at $50 each.

Nineteen-hundred-and-twenty-six was the propitious year that Casson was invited to join the Group of Seven, some four years

59   Maurice Cullen   *Spring Break-up, Cache River*   c.1914

after a founder member of the seven, Frank H. Johnston, decided to defect and pursue his own course as an artist. Casson seized the opportunity to bring the group back to strength. What he couldn't know was that one day it would elevate him to the olympian heights of being its last living member. It was a status and honour spontaneously acclaimed by collectors and speculators. This nostalgic hoopla soon generated startlingly high prices as people seemed willing to pay almost anything for his paintings. They now stand in line at his *vernissages* hoping for a chance to buy some little piece, and the total sale from these shows amounts to colossal sums. His public considers him a living god. But where were all these Johnnies-come-lately now buying Cassons as social pedigrees, when a few years earlier Group of Seven pictures were virtually impossible to dispose of?

To Casson's great credit this acclaim and wild speculation in his paintings has done little to change the splendid character of the man. Today, perhaps slightly bewildered by all the clamour and fuss, he remains as modest as ever. But I am sure it doesn't stop him from quietly enjoying the attention of a fickle public which clings to him as the last survivor of the legendary Seven.

Looking back over the years, I am warmed by the generosity and loyalty to their alma mater of a certain small group of Queen's graduates. It was astonishing to see what individuals such as Lorne Pierce, LLD, Dennis Jordan, M.D., D.I. McLeod the financier, and the lawyer Robert Segsworth, were able to do for their university. During the early 1940s, these people conceived the idea of building up a collection of fine Canadian paintings for Queen's University. Each of these men was distinguished in his own field and shared a common bond in the respect and regard which they held for their old university. They also possessed a special interest in art and therefore went to great pains to search out the best Canadian pictures they could then find. This was long before the days when there were tax write-off situations. To them it was simply a labour of love and a personal dedication. For years my father and I enjoyed a close association with Lorne Pierce and, through him, Dr. Dennis Jordan also became a good friend. I remember the mining lawyer Robert Segsworth when he lived in his Rosedale home full of fine furniture, Victorian bric-a-brac and pictures hanging two- and three-deep on the walls. The fourth member of this active group, D.I. McLeod the financier, was also a keen amateur artist who loved

60   Robert Pilot   *Late Winter, Perth, Ontario*   1930

to go on sketching trips with his professional artist friends. Nothing brought him more joy than to have his paintings selected and hung at the CNE or jury-judged shows. It gave him confidence and made him feel that his work counted.

As I recall events now, the first purchase of the Art Foundation was in 1941, with the acquisition of four Tom Thomson sketches. We had plenty of Tom Thomsons on hand at the time and the prices averaged $300 each. Since they were destined for a university, we allowed a discount of 10 per cent, bringing the cost of a Thomson sketch down to $270. Nineteen-forty-one was also the year when we bought all the J.W. Beatty estate pictures from the artist's widow. Lorne Pierce and Dr. Jordan selected for the university one of the Beatty's largest and finest canvases, *Winter, Bowen Island, B.C.*, at a cost of $540. A founding member of the university art committee, when Robert Segsworth died, he willed his collection to Queen's, to be turned over after his widow's death. It included another Beatty and a large interior study by Paul Peel as well as numerous European pictures. Then, in 1943, Thoreau MacDonald graciously made available to the Art Foundation the dramatic *Wild Ducks*, by his father J.E.H. MacDonald. The cost was $1,200. It took a lot of time and hard work to raise money during those early war years, as buying pictures either privately or for a university was not a popular pursuit. The value of these remarkable gifts in today's market would be hard to assess and, in quality, impossible to replace at any price.

It was about this time that I met the Swiss-born André Biéler, who was appointed in 1936 as Artist in Residence at Queen's University, succeeding the talented young Goodridge Roberts. By then a man of about forty years, Biéler applied for and got the job. His pictures weren't selling but with living accommodation supplied plus a salary and a small veteran's pension he had enough money to live on and buy painting materials. He was a fixture at Queen's University for the next twenty-seven years.

Unfortunately things did not run smoothly between the members of Lorne Pierce's volunteer art committee and Mr. Biéler. It seems that Biéler resented the fact that these amateur capitalists, whom he felt knew nothing at all about art, were presenting pictures to Queen's without his formal approval. Biéler became antagonistic and behaved more like an art czar than an art teacher. It

61 J.W. Beatty *Autumn, Algonquin Park* c.1915

was a situation which the art committee could not tolerate and it wasn't long before it withdrew its entire support. But Biéler's victory was a hollow one. Had he possessed a more sympathetic attitude in those days, Queen's University would have had even more rare and fine Canadian paintings for its permanent collection.

As a painter Biéler was a social realist. I think it shows up in one of his more attractive works, *Natalie, 1950*, in which he idealizes the figure of a young woman of the soil into a kind of rural madonna. Biéler was steeped in European traditions and his cultural roots lay deep in Switzerland and France. On several occasions he lent us pictures to sell but we could find no buyers for them. A restless individualist, Biéler possessed a good feeling for the work of other artists and invested wisely in Emily Carrs and other Canadian artists when prices were extremely modest. Later he sold some of them to good advantage.

Looking back on the 1940s, then, I would have to characterize it not as a decade of expansion but rather as a slow period of consolidation in our business. It would take another five years after the war for the economy to substantially improve and pictures to sell more easily.

8

The Beginnings of the Great Art Boom

The years between 1950 and 1960 represented for us a decade of much more significant growth than had the previous one. We increased the number of exhibitions by Canadian artists, and also showed more work by British and European painters. Sales steadily improved although there were still periods of financial drought when we sold hardly anything.

During the first ten years of the gallery's existence, until 1941, our best efforts produced sales of no more than $40,000 in one year but there were other twelve-month periods when we averaged less than half that amount. Another climactic eight years went by bringing us to 1950, the year we moved into our newly built gallery on Bloor Street West. By then the face of the world was looking more cheerful after five years of post-war recovery. Our total sales for 1950 reached the respectable sum of $81,000.

By 1951, after some years serving as trustee and chairman of the Toronto Board of Education, I decided to give up any last lingering thoughts of a personal political career. I then settled down to the task of finding further ways and means to expand a business I felt showed great potential for growth.

When my London partner Tom Baskett of P. & D. Colnaghi and Company and I took our first of many trips to western Canada beginning in September 1951, we were on the lookout for the work of promising local artists that we thought we could promote and sell in the east. We knew there were some neglected ones like Jack Markell in Winnipeg whose work we later showed in Toronto. We also searched out the director of the Coste House in Calgary, a pathetic little so-called art centre located in a house-gallery with no pictures in it. A dear man named Mr. Kee was in charge but he had no funds at all for buying pictures. However, he introduced us to one or two artists, including the Calgarian Maxwell Bates, but we instinctively knew his paintings would have no sales appeal in the east. We found not a single artist of promise in Edmonton at the time but in Vancouver we rather liked the work of Gordon Smith and Joseph Plaskett. Later, in 1956, A.Y. Jackson named Joseph Plaskett as his choice of the young Canadian artist who showed the greatest promise.

We continued to show work by some of the day's lesser known Canadian artists. For example there was the high spirited, Russian born painter, Paraskeva Clark, a harried housewife, who used to complain bitterly about her lack of painting time. She also felt discouraged by the general lack of appreciation for her work. In the spring of 1951, we exhibited some thirty-seven of Paraskeva's paintings but, from our point of view as well as hers, the show was an unmitigated disaster as we sold only four pictures at an average price of $60 each. Now, thirty years later, art historians have discovered her painting achievements and are arranging a large retrospective public exhibition of her work for 1982. Late though this be in the life of Paraskeva Clark, it will certainly assure her a niche in Canadian art history.

During the 1950s we held exhibitions by the emerging French Canadians, such as the talented Jacques de Tonnancour, the brilliant colourist Jean Paul Riopelle, Paul-Emile Borduas the abstract artist genius, and the gifted surrealist, Alfred Pellan. We gave Alex Colville, the magic realist painter then living in Saint John, New Brunswick, a showing in Toronto as early as 1958. Three of his pictures were sold, including one of a little girl skipping, and another of a lithe brown hunting dog wheeling in a field, two pieces typical of Colville where the viewer is caught up in the artist's rendition of a movement frozen in time and space.

We had more than two dozen uncatalogued exhibitions

62   Paraskeva Clark   *Still Life with Fruit*   c.1935

throughout the fifties by all the original members of the Group of Seven, Lawren Harris, J.E.H. MacDonald, Frank H. (Franz) Johnston, Arthur Lismer, Franklin Carmichael, A.Y. Jackson and even F.H. Varley. In addition, we held a Frank Hennessey exhibition, having acquired the pictures from his heirs. Then, in 1952, we purchased for $100 a large canvas by A.J. Casson, from the controversial publisher of the *Ottawa Citizen*, Harry S. Southam. Also on this same occasion we acquired from Mr. Southam other pictures by Frank Hennessey for exceedingly small sums.

In 1953 we bought from Varley his great *Summer in the Arctic* canvas and sold it the same year to a daughter of Charles S. Band for $900. Charlie Band was one of the early collectors of Emily Carr and had a close relationship with Group of Seven members A.Y. Jackson, Lawren Harris, and especially F.H. Varley. The greater part of the Band collection is now housed in the Art Gallery of Ontario. Since Band was a man with close ties to the Toronto gallery for many years (its president on two separate occasions), there would be no doubt that the important bulk of his collection would be left to what I think one could easily say was his favourite institution. In June 1980, I bought back the *Arctic* canvas at a public auction sale for $187,000.

In September 1955, a handsome young man with dark curly hair, wearing a pleasant grin, came into the galleries. He began his visit by noting that a current issue of *Time* Magazine suggested that paintings by the nineteenth- and twentieth-century French masters were not only beautiful to look at, but were probably excellent investments. (He was indeed years ahead of his time in this perception.) He enquired if we had any such pictures. It so happened that we had recently acquired in France a striking painting, *Fountain in Nice*, in cool greens and blues, by Raoul Dufy, and a typical Montmartre street scene by Maurice Utrillo. On my recommendation he bought the two for a total sum of $10,500; it turned out to be a brilliant buy, but also represented an awful lot of money in those days. He mentioned in passing that he was a practising physician in west Toronto and that his name was Dr. Morton Shulman. He also told me he had been lucky in buying and selling a West Coast pipeline stock and was anxious to reinvest some of his profits in good art. (During his first visit he made at least two quick calls to his stockbroker.) That was my first encounter with the irrepressible

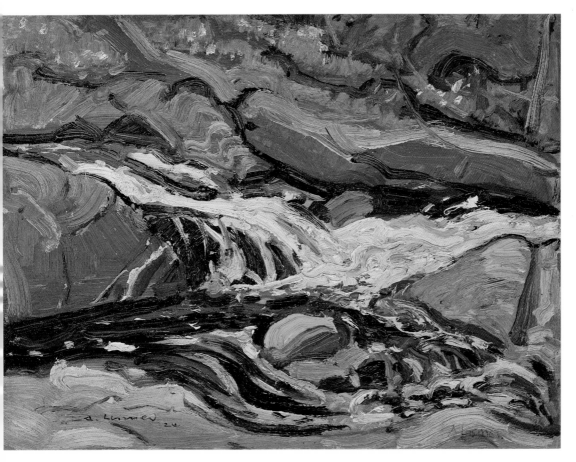

63   Arthur Lismer   *Rapids, Algoma*   1924

Dr. Shulman, many years before he became so well known as a politician, writer, and television personality.

Some months later, in March 1956, Dr. Shulman bought from us a marvellous little painting by Georges Rouault – a study of a tranquil old Parisienne writing; on another occasion he acquired an important canvas by Cornelius Krieghoff, one of the artist's *Settler's Log Cabin* series, for $7,500.

These were his first sallies into important art acquisitions and he writes complimentary things in his bestseller investment books concerning my efforts to advise him on good values in pictures. Some clients conveniently forget where and how they acquired their good pictures. Not Morty Shulman. A born collector, he later moved into other more exotic realms, like fine eighteenth-century watches and a little later still, into elegant examples of Russian Fabergé.

My father had a special interest in poetry and somewhere on his travels during the twenties met the Canadian poet Wilson MacDonald. Like the painters of those days, poets and writers also had a hard time earning a living, and Wilson MacDonald was more often than not in dire straits. He composed nostalgic, lyrical verse, much influenced by nineteenth-century romanticism.

In the late twenties, my father became an important patron of Wilson MacDonald and successfully organized some readings which the poet conducted with great *élan* and obvious delight. My role was to sell advertising space in special programs published to commemorate the events. But regardless of these modest successes Wilson MacDonald remained a bitter man, bitter first of all because he felt his poetry was insufficiently appreciated in Canada, and second because he was poverty-stricken. Medium in stature, he had querulous brown eyes, hands small like a woman's, and a narrow but prominent nose. His penmanship was the most exquisite I have ever encountered in my life; vastly superior even to the handwriting of George Thomson, our Canadian artist friend in Owen Sound.

It was my father's friendship with Wilson MacDonald that, in 1930, led to my visiting with Charles G.D. Roberts. Roberts lived at the time in the Ernscliffe Apartments, one of Toronto's early apartment blocks on Wellesley Street, in east-central Toronto. Mr. Roberts, I remember, possessed a patrician visage, was elegantly attired, and wore the large fashionable pince-nez of the day. He must

64   Arthur Lismer   *Little Islands, MacGregor Bay*   1929

have had a reasonably adequate income from his royalties. He was also very kind and had a roguish sense of humour. I felt honoured to have a chance to meet him because as a boy I had read some of his enthralling short stories set in the wilds of New Brunswick and Nova Scotia, in the public-school readers. Charles G.D. Roberts, greatly respected as a man of letters during his lifetime (he was knighted in 1935), is now regarded as the father of Canadian literature. It is said his writings, which expressed the euphoria aroused by Canada's Confederation, inspired a whole nationalistic school of late nineteenth-century Canadian poets.

During the war, about 1943, I got to know Theodore Roberts who was a poet and novelist like his brother Charles but not nearly as successful. Theodore approached us with an imaginative scheme to start up a new publication catering solely to the arts. As I recall now, it was to be a monthly journal featuring the works of poets, writers, and artists, solely Canadian in content. Both my father and I were intrigued with the idea especially because we felt it might help publicize Canadian art. But, alas, times were too hard and very little money for such a risky venture was forthcoming. Reluctantly, therefore, Mr. Roberts gave up his dream and shortly afterward withdrew from the Toronto scene.

The painter Goodridge Roberts sprang from the roots of what was probably the most famous literary family of the nineteenth-century Maritimes. His grandparents were early settlers in New Brunswick and his grandfather was one of those peripatetic Methodist ministers who toiled long and hard throughout his life over far-ranging parishes. Charles G.D. Roberts and Theodore were respectively Goodridge's uncle and his father. In his own art form Goodridge Roberts would one day far surpass his father's achievements as a writer, and later become just as famous in his painting métier as his Uncle Charles was in the field of Canadian literature.

Tall like his father, Goodridge Roberts was a loose-jointed, gangling figure of a man. He was dedicated to painting; his life was his art. A late starter, he didn't hit his true stride as a painter until the mid-1950s. A good part of his earlier life was taken up in teaching duties, primarily in order to subsist, because there was little sale for his paintings. Like the Impressionists before him he was also an *en plein air* painter. As he matured his work became more and more intense and colourful. He applied the paint to his pressed-board panels, either large or small, in a highly personal style with broad and mighty brushstrokes.

I remember a memorable visit with him in the late summer of 1956 at Calumet, Quebec, not far from the Oka Indian reserve. Here he owned a large property in the rolling foothills of the Laurentians which included an old farm house. Goodridge was devoted to the place and determined to try and stay there for at least a week or two during the spring and fall. On this occasion my wife and I were Joan and Goodridge's overnight guests and slept comfortably in the attic surrounded by dozens of his paintings. Each day he took to the fields with his easel and brushes and continued to produce an incredible number of works. When looking at one of these paintings you can almost smell the sweet odours from the grassy fields, a myriad of blades bowed by gentle breezes on the slopes, and sometimes imagine the more pungent scents of flowering weeds among them.

During this visit I ended up buying some thirty paintings. Like Paul-Emile Borduas, Goodridge offered incredibly high discounts on bulk buying. He priced his pictures according to size and on the present occasion voluntarily deducted 60 per cent from his basic price. He was yet another of those dedicated artists who had little use for money and as long as he could buy painting materials and feed and clothe himself and his wife, he was satisfied. The following morning we loaded the car with unframed paintings and incredible as it may seem the total cost amounted to only $7500.

By the early 1960s, Roberts had reached his full power as an artist and was producing a prodigious number of paintings. In fact he worked so hard and drove himself so relentlessly that his health became impaired; but nothing could make him slow down his frenzied zeal to paint. Goodridge Roberts' great idol was the painter Vincent van Gogh, and some of his later work possessed some of the reckless vitality that the great Dutchman attained in his work in his own final years. In the end Goodridge Roberts couldn't stand the pressure anymore and finally mental illness did him in at the age of seventy.

We also bought and exhibited the works of Stanley Cosgrove, an artist with original ideas, of French-Canadian-Irish descent. Cosgrove's earlier work has a fine enamel-like surface quality to it. He did still lifes, landscapes, with avenues of trees and figures of young women, full length and busts. Their faces often had a dream-like, ephemeral quality.

Jacques de Tonnancour was another splendid artist endowed with great energy and always searching for new ways to express his restless search for artistic truth. In the early 1940s, he had studied under Goodridge Roberts and was influenced by the Roberts' landscapes, later though Tonnancour went on to develop his own unique painter visions. Besides being one of our superior artists he is personally one of the finest individuals I have ever known. We held several exhibitions of his work during the late 1950s and he invariably came to Toronto for the openings. Jacques often stayed with us at our home and, possessing an uncommon sense of generosity, he once presented us with one of his large still life paintings as an outright gift.

Some time in 1956, I called on the young Harold Town when he worked in an upstairs studio in an old house on Rathnelly Street in midtown Toronto. I was interested in what he called his original single autographic prints. Like the dry points of David Milne, Town's prints were among the finest efforts by anyone practising the art of printmaking. Born in 1924, Town was a founding member of a short-lived but lively art movement called Painters Eleven. The story of this group has been well documented by the art historian Joan Murray. We held two superlative exhibitions by Harold Town, in 1959 and 1961. Both shows were enormously successful, and over a relatively short period of time we sold more than 100 of his pictures. Jerrold Morris was the organizer of these exhibitions and their remarkable success was the talk of the art community. Now, in 1982, the still productive Harold Town continues to exhibit. He is known not only as an artist but as a writer and provocative critic of the social scene.

By the mid-1950s we were averaging about seven exhibitions each season, and were providing showings in Toronto for many artists who had not exhibited here before. In fact, the 1950s was the beginning of the golden years of art dealing in both North America and Europe, and during that period, besides our Canadian exhibitions, we showed French, British, and Italian contemporaries, as well as sculpture by international masters. We were fortunate in having active English and European connections, while still maintaining a strong Canadian base.

65   Frederick H. Varley   *Summer in the Arctic*   c.1937

At this time the art scene was pulsating with many new art movements especially in the United States, France, and England, and fresh opportunities for art dealing seemed available everywhere. By 1957, my father and I concluded we needed another capable and energetic hand to join us. We decided to approach Jerrold A. Morris and invite him into the business as an associate. I had first met Jerry Morris in 1952 when he was curator of the Art Gallery of Vancouver and it was he who introduced us to the early Vancouver collectors, Thomas Ingledow and Mrs. James P. Fell. Later he moved to the San Francisco Museum of Art where he acted in a similar capacity. He didn't feel quite at home in the United States, however, and after some serious soul searching in 1957 decided to take up the challenge of a new position and return to Canada to work with the Laing Galleries. Jerrold Morris was a person dedicated to the world of art. As an art student and amateur artist, he had for many years collected photographs, prints and documents relating to every conceivable school of painting carefully providing rich historical background and other data. He also became a writer, and over the years produced several serious books on art subjects. He enjoyed working with artists and while with us organized a series of exhibitions of British Columbia artists, including B.C. Binning, Gordon Smith, John Korner, Takao Tanabe, and others.

Early in April 1959, we decided to explore the art scene in Paris so that we might consider the possibility of selling more contemporary French art in Canada. Through a former Morris colleague, Charles Sterling, curator at the Louvre Museum, Jerrold and I were put in touch with the director of the Museum of Modern Art in Paris, who responded by providing us with the names and addresses of nearly all the important artists living in and around Paris.

Our visits took us to nearly every section of Paris, including Montmartre, and even Vanves, where Riopelle had a studio. Some artists had studios in ancient buildings. Others worked from ateliers situated in dead-end streets. Through narrow accesses from the street we entered courtyards, our shoes crunching on the grey pebbled paths leading to the flats. Sometimes a drowsy concierge, startled by the noise, would cast us baleful looks. We ignored the challenge and just pressed on. Sometimes we toiled up flights of dark stairways only to discover the artist was absent. However, nearly all

66   A.Y. Jackson   *The St. Lawrence at St. Fidèle*   c.1928

the artists we did reach were co-operative and glad to show us their paintings.

Prices were reasonable in 1959, as most of these artists were unknown outside France and had little market. Even the great masters like Rouault, Utrillo, Braque, Vlaminck, Matisse, Dufy, Marquet, and Bonnard, all of whom had died in the late 1940s and the 1950s, were just becoming famous.

We spent about a week tracking down artists and the experience was rewarding. Finally we acquired enough pictures to provide what we thought would be a brilliant show for Toronto.

We bought large abstract canvases from the elegant Pierre Soulages, who was just then beginning to be recognized as a broad-brushed painter of importance. He drove us to his studio in a Citroen which floated like a cloud on its compressed-air suspension system. There was Maurice Brianchon, the patriarchal Parisian who painted attractive canvases somewhat in the manner of Bonnard, and lived in a luxurious flat in the centre of Paris. Also we met the convivial Jules Cavailles, a painter in the Matisse tradition who spontaneously invited us home for lunch, a rare complimentary gesture extended by a Frenchman on meeting two strangers for the first time. Every year following we received one of his signed coloured lithographs as a New Year's greeting. There were Gustave Singier and Alfred Manessier, two other colourful abstract painters, and we bought as well striking figures of circus clowns and chessmen, by Paul Aizipiri. The diminutive, sunny-dispositioned artist from Peking, Zao Wou-Ki, offered us abstracts with dreamy oriental overtones. We met the shy wisp-like figure Viera da Silva, a prominent Portuguese painter living in Paris. There were others like Bernard Dufour, Manoles Calliyannis, a tall, dark-haired young Greek, and the German expatriate Hans Hartung, a maimed veteran of the Second World War. With the possible exception of Brianchon, Soulages, and da Silva, the other artists were virtually unknown in North America.

We arranged to have the fifty-odd pictures we bought picked up by Lenars, our obliging Paris packers, and within three weeks they arrived safely by plane in Toronto. The total cost for the pictures, including packing and shipping charges, amounted to no more than $25,000. And this school of Paris collection resulted in

67   Paul Peel   *Femme au Jardin*   1889

one of the most colourful and attractive exhibitions we had ever assembled.

It is relatively easy to look back on events of the past and consider what one could have done differently to improve one's lot. I cannot help thinking, however, that if we had spent the same amount of time in New York as we had in Paris, and not much more money, we could have put together a smashing exhibition by the New York abstract expressionist school, for as it happened, most of the French painters whose works we bought then, are by now almost forgotten, having been overshadowed by their powerful contemporaries, the New York abstract expressionists.

It was the 1950s, then, that saw the fastest and greatest expansion of the Laing Galleries. This included an excursion into French classical and contemporary painting as well as sculpture, showing a strong selection of work by internationally renowned sculptors, many of whom were virtually unknown in Canada at that time.

9

In the Studios of Some Great Sculptors

In June 1955, I was in London, and while walking through Leicester Square, I dropped in at the Leicester Galleries to examine two curious-looking bronze objects which I had spied through the window. Instead of being cast in solid form, these pieces had large gaping holes through them. Although completely abstract they suggested the torso of the human figure. I asked one of the partners, Nicholas Brown, whose work they were. And that's how, quite by accident, the sculptor Henry Moore entered my life.

Henry Moore, the Yorkshireman, was then known only to a few *cognoscenti* in England and almost completely unknown elsewhere. The Leicester Galleries had been noted for nearly two generations for showing some of the great *avant-garde* French and British painters and sculptors in London and among whom was this man, Henry Moore. On the spur of the moment I bought the two Moore sculptures at a total cost of £140 sterling. This later proved to be one of the best hunches I had ever had.

There was at that time the problem of import duties. Alan Jarvis (a sculptor himself), when he was appointed director of the National Gallery of Canada in May of that year, soon successfully petitioned the government to remove these duties and taxes. From that point on, with the elimination of the duties we were able to ap-

171

proach sculptors direct with offers to buy and bring their works to Canada. It was Jarvis who had met Henry Moore when the former was living in England, and who arranged for me an introduction to Henry Moore in July 1956.

Moore lived in the village of Much Hadham in a lovely old white-washed cottage, called "Hoglands." There was a two-room, single-storey studio workshop adjacent. He used one room for the drawing and sculpting of small models and maquettes; the other for polishing and patinating the casts after their return from the foundry. The patina on his bronzes was important to Moore and he and his assistants spent a lot of time working on the desired finish.

Although living in the quiet country village of Much Hadham with his wife Irena, Henry Moore was also keenly aware of what was going on in the world about him. He knew the work of his contemporaries not only in England but in France and Italy as well. From his rather modest land holdings in the mid-fifties he went on to acquire additional ground and built other temporary studios way down in the fields and used them as extra places in which to work on some of his monumental-size pieces. As time went on, of course, some of these great casts were permanently placed in advantageous positions on his land. Moore, a man with a great feeling for posterity, especially in his old age (eighty-four this year), had planned to turn some of his acres into a gigantic sculpture garden featuring his work. Alas, people of the village objected because they were convinced throngs of visitors would ruin their quiet village life.

He also bought property that included an old farm building across the road where he stored many of his used original plasters. I think he had firmly decided by the mid-sixties that rather than destroy the plasters he would arrange for them to be preserved in some permanent collection. He told me that he felt these plasters represented himself as a sculptor more accurately than the actual bronze casts taken from them. The museum home he had in mind was eventually built in Toronto as the Henry Moore wing of the Art Gallery of Ontario.

Over the period of the fourteen or so years that I visited him, I suppose I got to know him as well as any outsider, and he seemed to enjoy my visits. My usual routine was to telephone him on arrival in London and arrange an appointment to see him. He was always most explicit about what train I should catch for Bishop's

Stortford. Having arrived there I would pick up a taxi for the short drive to Much Hadham through the fertile flat farmlands of Hertfordshire, usually arriving just in time for tea.

Mrs. Betty Tinsley was his long-time secretary and her job was not only to look after the correspondence but even more important to keep track of the number of casts made for each particular edition. There was always a waiting list for each piece he produced and in order to have a chance of getting one, it was essential to be on Mrs. Tinsley's list though, even then, you might lose out in favour of someone else's more urgent demand.

On many occasions, I was able to find a piece recently arrived from the foundry, and take delivery on the spot. I frequently found myself on the London train carrying these smaller pieces and drawing curious looks from the other passengers. Medium-sized bronzes such as those in his helmet head series were picked up at his studio later and sent on by air. But the largest and heaviest pieces came by sea.

On the thirty or so visits I made to see Henry Moore and buy his sculpture, I spent many instructive and interesting hours with the man and never, I think, came away empty-handed. (Back in 1957 I was still buying small bronzes from him which we then sold for as little as $240. Even in 1960, we were selling his sculptures in the $500-$600 range.)

Moore possessed the sense and drive of an early explorer in his search for ideas and new art forms from every available source. He studied everything: nature forms, pebbles and shells from the beaches, sun-bleached bones, early Greek and Roman bronzes in the British Museum, and complex stringed models used in geometric experiments seen in science museums. Nothing escaped the sculptor's keen eye.

When he spoke you were struck by the high timbre of his voice, which was greatly accentuated on the telephone line. It made him sound more like a soprano than the tough durable little Yorkshireman that he actually was. I found the strong Yorkshire accent retained from his boyhood both musical and pleasant. He was a man of exceeding good humour and his clear blue eyes frequently twinkled with merriment. Medium in stature with a strong frame, he had surprisingly small hands and it seemed slightly incongruous to see him working on those enormous pieces, some of which were always in progress. He was a prodigious worker, at times hewing from a massive piece of elm trunk a reclining figure in one studio, while in others he worked on six-foot-high plaster models. In the evenings he was usually found tinkering with new forms or making drawings in his "idea" studio. Like a painter he regularly used his small pieces as models or maquettes for medium and larger versions of similar subjects. He never paused in his constant search for new ideas.

It was never easy in the time allotted to get down to business with Henry. First there was the inevitable walk down the garden before tea time to see what was going on in the other studios. When I thought I saw something on hand I would enquire if a cast was available and his reply was invariably, "We must check with Mrs. Tinsley to see how the edition stands." It was almost impossible to get enough pieces together at one time for even a small show but we were still able, over a period of years, to acquire a large number of his bronzes. Moore once confided to me that he did not want hundreds of copies of his small sculptures floating around the art world. Yet demand caused the numbers in his editions to gradually increase from three or four to as many as twelve or more.

Money was unimportant to him and he spent little on himself personally. Time was his most precious commodity, and he husbanded it carefully. With his accumulating wealth he was able to increase his property holdings as well as finance the cost of the huge castings arriving at regular intervals from his English and European foundries.

Henry Moore struggled for years to keep his prices down but the pressure of demand for his work was relentless. Some people who bought from him almost immediately put their pieces into public auctions, realizing quick profits and rudely jolting his personal price scale.

He was also an acquisitive man and loved fine works of art both modern and ancient. He traded his sculpture to dealers for Post-Impressionist paintings and Italian Renaissance wood carvings. Of course this was good business for the art dealers as they made a double profit, first on the pictures they traded him, and then on the higher prices of Moore's increasingly popular sculpture.

At some point during the late fifties the Marlborough Gallery, London, became interested in Moore's work and Harry Fischer, an original partner, pressed Moore to allow him to market large pieces in continental Europe. Then, in 1969, Moore had two large simultaneous shows in New York; bronzes at Marlborough and abstract stone carvings in Italian marble at Knoedler's. The era of prodigious prices for his work was at hand, and Moore himself organized and orchestrated these exhibitions with admirable skill and enthusiasm.

By the mid-1960s Moore had become an international celebrity. He was hounded by countless dealers, collectors, publishers with editions of lithographs to sign, students to advise and just ordinary visitors. How he was ever able to continue turning out his vast production of sculpture is a mystery I will never be able to solve.

Henry Moore reveled in the acclaim that followed his exhibitions in foreign countries. He enjoyed selling to individuals like the notorious multi-millionaire uranium king, Joseph Hirshhorn. Mr. Hirshhorn entertained Henry with his brash antics and Brooklyn-Yiddish accent. He also sold to my friend John MacAulay of Winnipeg, the large *Internal External Forms* piece for $15,000 which he had originally promised to me, but to make up for it he let me have the final cast, number three, of his famous 1951 *Festival Figure*.

During the spring of 1981, a colossal exhibition of his large sculptures, maquettes, drawings, and lithographs opened in a magnificent park in Madrid, to the great acclaim of the critics. It has been suggested that art is never beyond politics and I don't think it is commonly known that Henry Moore was one of the surrealist group in England that signed a manifesto in the mid-thirties deploring the British government's policy of non-intervention in the Spanish Civil War. But the Spaniards have long memories and Moore, along with Robert Motherwell, the American abstract impressionist, are both considered heroes among the intellectual and artistic elite of Spain.

I still think of Moore as one of the great entrepreneurs of the mid-century. He will leave his sculpture as his memorial. In my opinion it will be up to future generations to fully assess its worth and to determine Moore's final place in art history.

An occasion that stands out in my mind is my first meeting with Dame Barbara Hepworth, at her home in St. Ives, Cornwall. I had taken the long overnight train ride from London, and after freshening up and having a light breakfast at one of the local hotels,

I set off to see her. The studio stood on the side of a steep hill and I arrived there with my taxi about ten. I was met at the front door by a magnificent woman wearing a kerchief, who invited me in. It was Barbara Hepworth, then in her middle fifties. A little later she led me into the most beautiful sculpture garden I had ever seen, filled with her bronzes, alabasters, and white marbles. Situated among palm trees it overlooked the Bay of St. Ives. Barbara Hepworth and her garden proved an overwhelming experience.

Just across the ancient narrow street from her front door she had acquired another building called "Le Palais de Dance," ever mindful that it was formerly a popular dance hall in St. Ives. Its walls were painted stark white. Here she housed some of her larger interior pieces.

Born in Yorkshire in 1903, she was five years younger than Henry Moore, and joined him in 1918 at the Leeds School of Art as a scholarship student. She had been married to two artists but was now living on her own. Her first husband was John Skeaping, also a sculptor, by whom she bore a son, and the second was the famous Ben Nicholson with whom she had triplets.

For me, she possessed a special kind of magnetism, and photographs from her youth remind one of the face of a pre-Raphaelite madonna. As time went on she looked upon me more as a friend than as a businessman buying and selling sculpture, and her smoky brown eyes would glow like orbs when we talked about her sculpture.

She was also a woman who loved a party. I remember her renting a magnificent suite at the Great Eastern Hotel, Liverpool Street Station, for an elegant buffet luncheon prior to the opening of her great retrospective exhibition of sculpture at the Tate Gallery, in 1969. Nearly everybody active in the contemporary art world came to the opening to pay her homage. The show proved a great triumph for Hepworth. When I appeared at her party in semi-formal attire, she exclaimed, to my delight and embarrassment, that I looked "smashing." She was a person of wit with a vital and alert mind, and we enjoyed a good rapport. Enormously ambitious to be recognized as the great sculptor she was, Barbara was always eager to show in as many public exhibitions as possible and indeed won high acclaim in numerous international sculpture shows.

Dame Barbara Hepworth was, I believe, intellectually as

brilliant and technically just as great and fine a sculptor and innovator as Henry Moore. She didn't quite possess the range of his bronzes or elm-wood and stone carvings, but in purity of form her smooth and harmonious stone carvings are unrivalled. Hepworth and Moore, it is said, discovered and explored the use of the hole in sculpture; they found this a release of sculptural tension, and also a rest for the eye. Barbara Hepworth made small polished bronze motifs 3″ or 4″ tall, as well as great marbles from 7′ to 10′ in height. She also executed seductive alabaster carvings in abstract forms. She enjoyed carving in wood, but we soon four.d from experience that her wood carvings tended to warp and split in the dry Canadian atmosphere, if they arrived in Canada with even a hint of a crack in them. In addition Barbara was a fine painter and draftsman. But it should be added that being a sculptor was not an easy profession for a woman to pursue. During the twenties and continuing for two more decades she received little recognition. Sales were pitifully few, there were the children to be looked after, and little money was available for even the simplest things in life. She lived by accepting small commissions and selling a few drawings.

Barbara Hepworth was supremely conscious of the value of her sculpture as works of art and always knew precisely the market value of her work. For example, if the pound sterling had shrunk on the international money market in terms of the dollar from sales she had made a few months previously, she would raise her prices to take care of any exchange loss.

Dame Barbara was still producing some of the best things of her life when she was struck down with cancer but she rallied and continued to work to the end. She died in 1975 from the effects of smoke fumes in her bedroom during a fire, probably caused by a burning cigarette. She left her garden and property to the town of St. Ives as a museum for her sculpture.

Jacob Epstein was a compulsive collector who had acquired a large collection of African wood carvings and masks. Though born in the United States, he lived in Hyde Park Gate, in those days, just opposite the London town house of Winston Churchill. It was in London that I got to know him.

Epstein always had a bronze head of Peggy Jean, or another of his attractive child subjects, sitting on the top of his grand piano. If you enquired whether you could buy it he would

177

nod his head and quote a price of approximately £100. The next time you visited him it would have been replaced with another cast of a similar subject, equally appealing. Epstein didn't bother to record the total number of casts he made of any one subject and as far as he was concerned they were all originals. I bought a large number of bronzes from him including portraits of his wife Kathleen, Dierdre, and his marvellous head of Albert Einstein.

I had become very interested in sculpture as an art form and in its sales possibilities in Canada. One day in 1958, I asked Henry Moore whom he considered the most important sculptors in Europe. He suggested that two of the best were the Italians, Marino Marini and Giacomo Manzu, both of whom had studios in Milan.

For many years the Hotel Savoy boasted as its head barman a celebrated Irishman, by the name of Joe Gilmore. He was the affable confidant of peers of the realm, of thriller writers and other novelists, of actors, bankers, and moneymen from the City – indeed of business tycoons from all over the world. On hearing of my proposed trip to Italy, Joe immediately suggested I should get in touch with his friend Angelo who was his opposite number at Milan's elegant Principe Savoie hotel. Angelo was the distinguished president of the International Bartenders Guild and enjoyed greeting his customers in the hotel's main lobby, dressed in immaculate midnight-blue tuxedo trousers surmounted by an elegant off-white dinner jacket trimmed with gold buttons and braid. Indeed, Angelo, a tall, northern Italian, looked more like the aide-de-camp to a five-star general, or the general himself, than a barman.

Like the magnificence of his garb, Angelo turned out to be a jewel of a person. He had learned English from the Americans during the war and gave me the most gracious assistance possible. He telephoned Marino Marini but the sculptor was not available as he was just returning home to Milan from Locarno. And there was no answer at the Manzu studio. I therefore decided to stay in Milan for an extra day or two and have a look at some of the city's private galleries. It was on this occasion that I met Carlo Cardazzo, a dealer in contemporary Italian art. Cardazzo was a patrician sort of fellow who had lost a leg at Bengazi in 1942, ending up as a prisoner of war. He personally owned a fine collection of drawings and paintings by Modigliani. He had two good artist friends, Gentilini and Cappogrossi, and insisted on taking me to their studios to have a look at their work. I liked it and a few weeks later in Toronto we had rather a successful joint exhibition of their paintings. Looking back to those times, I regret not having seen more of this unusual man Cardazzo. He made a lasting impression on me even though our paths crossed but briefly. Sadly he died shortly afterwards.

The following morning I set out by taxi for Manzu's studio on the off-chance that I might find him at home. The building was a dull and sombre looking one-storey cement structure surrounded by a solid wall with an entrance through an iron gate. Having arrived at the front door, I was greeted amicably by a pleasant woman of ample proportions who immediately motioned me to come in. She spoke no English at all but had a natural ability to communicate in sign language. Clasping her hands together near the point of her chin, she suggested prayer, then with uplifted arms she traced a tall headdress, or bishop's mitre, and repeated the phrase, *"Professore Manzu – il Papa, Roma."* I soon caught the drift of her message, that Manzu must be in Rome waiting on the Pope. Indeed I later learned that he had been commissioned by Pope John XXIII to create a set of bronze doors for St. Peter's featuring biblical themes in bas-relief, and was also working on a head of the Pope.

She then placed a telephone call, and almost immediately a young man appeared who introduced himself as Pio, the sculptor's son. He took me to look around his father's studio and, in what was otherwise a bare and austere room, I became conscious of some simply magnificent pieces. This was the very first time I had ever set eyes on the sculpture of Giacomo Manzu, and I found it a moving experience. There were at least fifteen works, ballerinas with pony tails, skaters, seated cardinals in flowing robes, and busts of young women. It was with a feeling of wonder and awe that I found myself entering Manzu's world of sculpture without having yet met the man.

Contemporary sculpture was not selling in Italy during those years and Manzu was sending most of his work to England and Germany. He had no dealer commitments in North America but intimated someone in New York was interested in buying his work. I enquired of Pio if some of the pieces might be for sale and could hardly believe my ears and good luck when he said, "Yes," assuring me his father would write me as soon as possible, quoting prices and other pertinent information.

Sure enough, a couple of weeks following my return to Toronto, I received a letter from Manzu, expressing regret that he had not been at home to meet me and enclosing a price list of the pieces I had seen in his studio. We were thus able to begin a successful business association that was to last for a good number of years. On my next trip to Italy, I got to meet Manzu personally. Born in Bergamo in 1908, the twelfth child of an impoverished family, whose father was a shoemaker and church sexton, Manzu was then about fifty years of age. His was a stocky figure and he usually wore a hat to conceal his baldness. Vital and intense as he certainly was, I always found him quietly friendly. By 1960, he had moved to Rome and on various occasions he drove me to his home and studio on the outskirts of the hallowed city.

The following year, I was in Vevey, a small place near Lausanne where my daughter Andrea was attending Le Grande Verger School, having enrolled there to learn French. The school was situated on a beautiful piece of land that gently sloped towards a lake and was conducted by a portly old Swiss schoolmaster, more of a disciplinarian, I suspect, than a scholar. The young lady students came from all over the world – England and continental Europe, North, Central and South America, Egypt and Iran. Whatever knowledge Andrea was able to acquire at the school was enriched by the friendships she made with other students and kept through the years.

It was the end of the term before the summer holidays, and I thought it would be a good contribution to my daughter's general education as well as a pleasant experience, if she could have the chance of meeting some of the famous Italian sculptors with whom I had been dealing and see them at work in their studios.

From Lausanne we took the train to Milan. On arrival there our first visit was to Marino Marini and his wife Marina who lived in a modern apartment across from a courtyard where Marino had his working studio. Nearby was a small bronze foundry which had existed since the fifteenth century. There are a surprising number of ancient bronze foundries still going strong in Italy. Marini's studio contained some finished bronzes with their typical powdery patinas as well as plasters and armatures ready to receive the clay or plaster. Marino was a medium tall, northern Italian, born in Tuscany in 1901. He had one of those highly malleable faces with a wide mouth that could break out into a grin or produce loud peals of laughter; a garrulous creature, not reserved like Manzu, a man he, in fact, considered his rival. His wife Marina was a beautiful and distinguished lady. She spoke good English and looked after her husband's correspondence.

By the early fifties his work was just beginning to become known outside Italy and it was being shown in New York by the avant-garde former German dealer Curt Valentin, who also handled the work of Henry Moore. On occasion the Marinis invited me to their lovely villa by the sea at Forte dei Marmi, near Carrara. Sometimes Marini polychromed his sculpture in the brightest of hues which I personally found bizarre and unattractive. A distinctive white powdered patina characterized the finish of his broad, heavy-hipped female figures and horse and rider subjects. As a younger sculptor he did some superb marble busts in a naturalistic style. But it was his horses with their mounts, or single-horse sculptures that propelled his name into the centre of the international art world. I bought many pieces large and small from this entertaining clown prince of Italian sculptors. By the late sixties Marini had become wealthy but unfortunately also unproductive. He was indifferent to the pleas of dealers and amateurs to sell them his work.

The next day Andrea and I took the Rapido to Rome where I planned to see my friend Giacomo Manzu and acquire more of his unique bronzes. These were unique in their classical sense of beauty and also because Manzu produced only one cast of each subject. We arranged to meet the following day for dinner. Early the next evening Manzu, with his friend Inge (who was our driver on this occasion), picked us up in their Fiat at the Hotel Excelsior on the Via Veneto and took us to dine in one of his favourite restaurants in the centre of old Rome. Afterwards we went on an extensive trip through the grand and ancient city. It was a warm, showery evening and the tour, which didn't end until nearly midnight, was an exultant experience as well as an aesthetic adventure. Manzu had met Inge, a young dancer, and the great love of his life, for the first time in 1954, during a teaching engagement in Salzburg at the Summer Academy. Inge had a Nordic-type beauty with a finely contoured face, high cheekbones, and the figure of a robust ballerina. He fell madly in love with her and that year did the first of a long series of pencil, pen and ink and watercolour drawings of her, soon followed by magnificent bronze busts.

Manzu viewed the sights of Rome through the three-dimensional eyes of a sculptor and the Italian side of his nature burst with pride when he pointed out the wonders of the city to us. He knew the historical background, the name of the sculptor or architect of every monument or building of distinction in Rome, and he became more and more animated as he talked about them. He showed us architectural masterpieces hidden away in small *piazzas* in the inner city and called Bernini's fountains the quintessence of high Baroque. He escorted us to the Capitoline, Rome's ancient capital, to see the equestrian statue of Marcus Aurelius, which looked strikingly eerie under the lights as raindrops splashed on the horse's back. The 1,700-year-old bronze statue of the emperor astride his horse has remained the centrepiece of the Capitoline since Michaelangelo moved it there from the Forum in 1538. Manzu regarded it as the only early Roman bronze of its era to survive the melting pots of the Popes, then intent on Christianizing Rome. In 1981 the giant figure of Marcus Aurelius was lifted off his eleven-foot-high horse and the two pieces were placed on separate vehicles and paraded through the city. That was the final bow to the Roman populus before being transported to a special studio for restoration. The statue, say the Italian experts, is now so badly eroded and weakened from the effects of sulphur fumes since the last world war that it may never be returned to its former place of glory outdoors in the great *piazza*.

Manzu kept us in rapt attention, but it was Inge, fluent in both Italian and English, who made it possible for us to comprehend and appreciate his remarkable commentary on the wonders of Rome. It was a memorable evening!

In the late fifties, I also bought bronzes from Giuseppe Mazzullo, Pericle Fazzini, and Pietro Consagra. Consagra, whose sculptures were linear in form, something like cut-outs in bronze, was married to an American woman, who acted as our interpreter. Another sculptor, who lived just outside Rome in a villa with a handsome courtyard, was Emilio Greco. He specialized in sculptures of long-limbed girls with small breasts made to look even smaller under tightly drawn bodices. These female figures were repeated in sizes that varied from twelve inches to seven feet. Perhaps they were a little stagey but they were beautifully modelled and attractive to look at. He also did many busts of female subjects.

Some of these Italian sculptors became my friends and for several years I visited them and brought their work to Canada where they were much admired.

The American sculptor, Alexander Calder, lived in quite a different kind of world. He invented what he called the "mobile," a kind of kinetic sculpture with thin flat pieces of metal cut like silver or bronze fishing lures; others were brightly coloured. They were well engineered and delicately balanced on fine metal wire fanning out from a central axis on branches and left free to move or sway in a soft breeze.

By 1962, I had heard a lot about Alexander Calder and wanted to meet him personally and if possible buy some of his work. It so happened that my friend Barbara Hepworth knew him well and she gave me a letter of introduction. He was known to her as "Sandy."

By the early 1960s, Calder was spending much of his time working in France. I had recently seen an exhibition of his work at the Museum of Modern Art in Paris and was delighted by his skilful and imaginative fashioning of animals and characters of the circus including clowns and trapeze artists. I was convinced that I was looking at an unusual talent, someone who could cut, bend, and twist plain wire into most appealing art forms.

In any event, I telephoned Calder's home from Paris and talked to his wife Mary, who arranged an appointment to meet her husband the following day. They lived in the Loire Valley near Tours and I took the train there the next morning. After picking up a taxi at the station I was driven six or seven miles through the lovely wine-growing country to his cottage across from a small river and millpond.

A formidable high iron gate with a menacing sign forbidding uninvited visitors to trespass effectively barred the way, and even though I had an appointment I still had a feeling I was trespassing. And just in case Calder had changed his mind about seeing me and taking no chances of being stranded in some hostile place, I asked my driver to stand by and I finally decided to push open the gate. I was proceeding inside on the gravel path when I observed a hulking figure of a man with a shock of white hair slowly ambling toward me. After coolly sizing me up he greeted me, with a gruff but not unfriendly air, and invited me inside.

It was a limestone cottage once owned by a vintner and probably built early in the seventeenth century. The main room, actually the only room of consequence, was dominated by an old refectory table about twelve feet in length. At the left was a small workshop where several unfinished mobiles were suspended from the ceiling and two or three small "stabiles" stood on the table.

After a bit we walked into the garden brilliant with June flowers but otherwise unkempt. We then proceeded to his painting studio, a crude outbuilding, where he showed me some of his new tempera paintings. They were reminiscent of the work of Joan Miro, another friend of Calder's. These temperas, or gouaches, were painted on heavy hand-made paper and were as colourful as the flowers in his garden. We then walked to the crest of a small hill to visit an enormous barnlike studio he had constructed to work on his "stabiles." The fabrication of these large pieces was completed by welders and metal workers at a foundry in nearby Tours.

When we returned to his cottage, it was already late morning. "Would you like to see my wine cellar?" he asked. Approximately fifteen paces from his cottage was a deep cavern cut out of the solid rock, lit by a single, dim electric lamp. It contained thousands of bottles of white wines of the Loire. This cellar was also centuries old, probably carved out of the hill by the original wine grower owner himself. Sandy then picked out three bottles of wine and carried them inside, amiably slamming them down on top of the table, all the while attracting withering glances from his wife who, by then, had returned from a trip to the village. He then proceeded to open the bottles. From a nearby cupboard he produced two large tumblers and began to pour. I will never forget his strange way of pouring wine. Instead of holding the bottle near the base in the normal way, he chose instead to grasp it at the neck and his hand shook so badly that I thought for sure he would shatter the glasses. Somehow he filled them without a disaster.

Calder had no mobiles for sale at the time and I had not been at all interested in his stabiles, even if some had been available. However, in the end I bought about twenty of his fresh, colourful gouache paintings. He rolled them into a large loose bundle, which he secured with a cord. And, handing it to me, he said I could pay him later.

Altogether it had been a delightful and singular encounter. Sandy Calder and his wife then drove me to Tours where we lunched in a restaurant overlooking the old town square. After lunch I caught the train for Paris, completely convinced that I had spent the day with another creative genius.

It was in November 1959, that we held what was probably our most innovative and successful exhibition during the 1950s' decade. It was not a selection of paintings, however, but a collection of fifty pieces of sculpture together with thirty drawings and watercolours by the same sculptors. Good sculptors are also competent draftsmen and often do numerous drawings and compositions before proceeding to model in clay or plaster. Indeed a sculptor can move naturally from sculpture to painting and back again as if one is an extension of the other. Called "Sculpture – Ten Modern Masters," it was the first exhibition of its kind in Canada, and comprised the work of ten important international sculptors, including Jacob Epstein, Henry Moore, Barbara Hepworth, Marino Marini, and Giacomo Manzu.

Sculpture has been called a neglected art of the twentieth century and the sculptors had taken a back seat to the painters, but finally things were beginning to change in their favour. Up until then, these sculptors had had no connection with any art dealers in Canada, and we became the first commercial gallery in the country to exhibit and sell their work.

68 James W. Morrice *The Market Place, St. Malo* c.1902

10
Reflections on a Career

During these days, more often than not, I find myself referred to as a dealer-collector. I don't mind the label – in fact it is an apt one.

It was largely my fascination with the work of James W. Morrice, the nomad Montreal-born painter-genius, which carried me over that hazardous line from dealer to collector. I bought his paintings at every opportunity, finding them in the United States, England, France, Toronto, and Montreal. I developed a passion for his work from the time I saw it in an exhibition of his paintings at our gallery in 1934, and began my own collection of his pictures in 1950. I had also by then personally acquired paintings by Tom Thomson, J.E.H. MacDonald, and David Milne at a time when they cost almost nothing.

In my first book I talked a lot about the above-mentioned artists. But the main theme concerned various phases of the art business, prices of pictures, and the art market in general. In the present book I have tried to reveal more of my personal feelings for art and artists, and examine as well further aspects of the art world; for example, the impact of significant nineteenth-century Canadian art discoveries recently made in England and Scotland.

Long have I enjoyed pictures from diverse schools and different lands, not only the Vermeers and Hobbemas, but smaller masters like the Karel du Jardins or the van der Heydens, all creations made during Holland's stupendously rich seventeenth century. I have delighted in nineteenth-century France's munificent harvest of painters, the Monets and Cézannes, but that doesn't stop me from equally enjoying flower studies by Fantin Latour, or Boudin's enticing beach scenes. Savouring the masters is rather like drinking a vintage Château Lafite; there is still plenty of room left for enjoying wines of less noble growth.

It is interesting to note that throughout my life in the picture business, and even today, people still ask me, out of genuine interest and curiosity, whether I draw or paint myself. They seem to take it for granted that an art dealer by virtue of the nature of his business is probably also a painter. Some dealers are indeed artists, but for me the answer is no; I don't draw or paint at all. However, probably the next best thing to being an artist is having the opportunity to deal in good art. But you don't learn about art the same way you are taught astronomy, or for that matter, the history of art at a university. The learning process I refer to relates to having an inherent feeling for a piece of art. Having a good eye for a picture is rather like being born with a good ear for music; you either possess it or not, because this sensibility can rarely be instilled in a person.

There is a surprisingly prevalent belief among many people, otherwise intelligent and sensitive, that the quality of a work of art has a lot to do with the age of the object. On many occasions individuals have brought in pictures for me to examine, which are obviously old, and are surprised and disappointed to learn that age has little to do with either commercial or aesthetic value. Inevitably they heave a sigh of resignation while still justifying their original conviction that the pieces in question must be valuable and good because they have been in the family for a generation or more.

Connoisseurship, I have discovered, comes only after a long period of taking hard and loving looks at fine pictures and finding that after a while the pictures begin to communicate by smiling back at you. When you really find pictures staring at you, then you truly are a connoisseur. It may seem odd for me, a lifelong dealer, to admit I admire the connoisseur as a man who prefers pictures to money. At the same time I am also very much aware that one needs to have the money to buy them.

During my art dealing career I can remember a number of people who were blessed with the ability to recognize the quality of a

69   Tom Thomson   *Spring Ice and Birches*   c.1916

picture outside its own context. What I mean is, the capacity to judge quality in isolated examples of an artist's work. This aptitude is, of course, greatly enhanced by the study and exposure to good art, but without some natural perception the ability to assess quality in the visual arts could hardly mature. I have known individuals who have attempted art dealing as a trade or profession, but have failed because they were unable to learn how to assess the quality of pictures, plus the fact that they had no feeling at all for the business. How does one determine that mysterious thing called quality in judging a drawing, painting, or a piece of sculpture? A professor of philosophy or aesthetics might make a stab at an answer but his pronouncement would probably obscure the art. I believe judgement of art is an instinctive thing, an involuntary response, an authentic emotion, or a nerve-tingling sensation. As a picture dealer I admit this emotion is much stronger and more positive if it concerns a work of excellence that I am hoping to buy, rather than if it were an Old Master hanging on the walls in some remote museum. The excitement is greater when related to the sense of quest and quarry.

Somehow, however, I always return to my first love, the art of Canada. It is not easy to explain this phenomenon, as I am no flaming nationalist, but there quietly exist emotional factors within me that draw me like a magnet to the art and artists of my own native land.

I am often asked whom I consider to be Canada's ten greatest artists. This is of course a subjective matter, but for the sake of discussion I will go out on a limb by naming my ten personal choices for this nebulous but highly vaunted honour. The temptation is to do it chronologically – starting with the two nineteenth-century artists Paul Kane and Cornelius Krieghoff, to each of whom I have devoted a chapter – but that would be hedging.

My first choice is James W. Morrice (1865-1924), Canada's great Post-Impressionist. He made paintings say things that were never said before or after. The breadth and originality of his subject matter and the seductive colours of his palette seem to place him beyond reach of most mere mortal artists. He painted exotic places in North Africa, like Marrakesh, Tangiers, and Algiers, also Cuba and the West Indies. In Quebec he celebrated the arrival of winter by painting a final trip of the ferry boat steaming across the St. Lawrence through the ice floes, before arctic blasts froze the mighty ri-

70   J.E.H. MacDonald   *Pump and Pumpkins – A Sunny Corner*   1916

71   Lawren Harris   *Trees and Hill, Algoma*   1919

72   David B. Milne   *Across from the Garage, Palgrave*   1930

ver. I also love his work for its rendition of something of the peace and harmony of the Edwardian era, the opulent decade that began the century. Vignettes of Paris streets and parks with figures, the coastal towns and seaside views of Normandy and Brittany are the stuff his pictures are made of, all done in a style so personal and hauntingly reflective as to make his art seem timeless.

Tom Thomson (1877-1917) is my next choice. The reason – because he was such a smashing colourist, cramming into the final three years of his life some of the most dramatic studies of the northern bush and wind-swept lakes created by any artist anywhere.

Number three is J.E.H. MacDonald (1873-1932), the poet and elder sage of the Group of Seven, who in his Thornhill and Algoma periods (a total span of some twelve years) produced perhaps the most elegant work of any Canadian painter. Just look at the sketches reproduced in this book, *Pump and Pumpkins* and *Cliffs Near Hubert, Algoma*, to confirm it. His vibrant vermilion colours commemorate his great Algoma painting years.

I salute Lawren Harris (1885-1970) as my fourth choice. It was he who organized the first box-car trip to Algoma in September 1918. His paintings of Toronto street scenes and old houses in Ontario villages, miners' houses in Cape Breton, done during the teens of the century, are alone striking enough to perpetuate his name in Canadian art history. His Algoma and north shore Lake Superior sketches are epics of their kind and add further to his lustre, as do the paintings from his Arctic trip of 1930. We are proud to have acted as his agent for thirty-five years.

My fifth choice is David Milne (1882-1953), whom I got to know personally from 1934 to 1938, when he was holding annual exhibitions with us. I took note of his fresh new way of seeing nature, and in conversations with him absorbed some of his painting philosophy. One of his aesthetic theories was that all but the essential elements of a composition should be omitted. He called it a shorthand style. Milne was also Canada's finest printmaker. His dry point etchings alone have given him world-class status.

My next choice is Cornelius Krieghoff (1815-1872), until recent times downgraded in certain circles as a minor product of the Dutch and Düsseldorf Schools – a completely erroneous assumption. Well schooled as he certainly was in his youth, he became a master of his technique and turned into a truly original artist. He was a su-

73 Cornelius Krieghoff *The Habitant Peddler* c.1860

74   Paul Kane   *Buffalo Grazing, Indian Summer Near Fort Carlton*   c.1846

perb colourist and superior draftsman with a Rabelaisian sense of humour, and his paintings had a unique flavour surpassed by no other artist on the North American continent at the time. Without Kreighoff's painting contribution, which reached heroic proportions, Canada's legacy of nineteenth-century art would be grievously poorer.

I choose next Paul Kane (1810-1871), because he was, more than any other artist, the father of Canadian art. The sheer scope of the territory he covered during his epic 1846-48 trip to Ruperts' Land and the Pacific, along with the colourful and creative work he accomplished during the journey, is enough to stagger the imagination. The quality and range of subject matter in the hundreds of sketches, small paintings, and field studies of Indian tribes, remain one of the great artistic achievements of the nineteenth century.

A.Y. Jackson (1882-1973), my eighth choice, was probably the most prolific as well as one of our best Canadian artists who, during a long life, must have painted at least 4,000 pictures. In my opinion, his most striking works are the colourful French-Canadian farm and village scenes of the 1920s and early 1930s. Picturesque, and painted in the Post-Impressionist style, which he learned in France, they are poignant reminders of the social and cultural significance of the Quebec rural communities of that time.

Although not the first to paint the village life and farmsteads of Quebec (James W. Morrice, Clarence Gagnon, and to some extent Maurice Cullen and Horatio Walker, had painted similar subjects years before), Jackson with his sympathetic look at rural French Canada remains the best known. For more than two decades between the Great Wars, and later, he did hundreds of oil sketches in Quebec and filled his sketch pads with numerous pencil drawings.

Whatever sketches Jackson sold in those early days, he sold in Toronto, a few to the National Gallery in Ottawa, and some through the Montreal dealers Scott and Sons and William Watson. His Quebec village landscapes possessed a special appeal for English Canadians. Hardly any were bought by the French Canadians. Indeed Quebeckers of the present generation view such pictures as quaint clichés, quite anachronistic in the social and cultural history of their province.

75 A.Y. Jackson *A Quebec Village* c.1929

76 Emily Carr *The Red Stump* c.1934

My next and ninth choice is the West Coast painter Emily Carr (1871-1945). The magnificent series of fauvish Indian community houses and totem pole subjects of her immensely productive visit of 1912 to the Queen Charlotte Islands, after her return from France, would be enough to enshrine her forever among our greatest artists. But, in addition, there was a significant series of British Columbia forest interiors, primeval and mysterious, which came later. Unlike many artists, Emily Carr could handle the rich greens of her mighty rain forests. She also painted striking views of the isolated spindly trees, worthless as timber, she explained, and left uncut by the loggers, which proudly reached their green-swatched heads high into the sky.

My tenth choice, and the only abstract painter on my list, is Paul-Emile Borduas (1905-1960), the ex-patriate French Canadian, whom I met in Paris early in 1956. He was one of the few abstract artists whose work I really liked and which struck a chord within me. Over the next four years we bought so many paintings from Borduas that we probably were the main source of his livelihood. A forlorn and lonely figure, he was the last of our great painters to die poor and practically unsung. I felt a great compassion for the man. Non-objective as they were, his paintings from the early fifties remind me of birch groves, maple-sugar bush stands, or autumn hardwoods, their colours reflected in a stream or lakeside. Borduas continued to instil his art forms with the impressions and the nostalgic vision of boyhood days in St. Hilaire, Quebec.

Then there were the bold, resonant paintings of his final years; jagged rectangles, or semi-rectangular forms of black or dark brown floating intrusively on a background of pure white. While I personally prefer the harmony of his earlier canvases, the latter paintings, severe and powerful as they are, will probably remain Borduas' most important painting creations.

In presenting this list, I know full well that I have omitted some famous names. A lot, of course, depends on one's point of view, whether one is a dealer, artist, collector, art historian, or someone just interested in art. Although I stand committed to my own selection I can't help thinking how interesting it would be to gaze into a crystal ball and see how the pundits half a century hence will judge Canada's artists of this period.

I am quite firm, however, in the knowledge that for most

77   Paul-Emile Borduas   *Légers Vestiges d'Autumn*   1956

of my life art has humbled and awed me; I revel in its beauty, using the word "beauty" in the old-fashioned sense of truth and harmony. Throughout my five decades in the art world, I have watched generations of Canadian artists battling in their lifetime for deserved recognition. I have seen first hand the lukewarm reception they have received in their own country. It is worth rejoicing at the recent heartwarming change in attitude towards the arts in Canada. Now artists can immediately sell out the contents of their studios for huge sums. Indifference is giving way to acclaim, and ignorance is being dethroned by further education and appreciation – a good omen for the future.

Indices

Colour Plates

PLATE 20
Edward M. Richardson
Gold Mining in the Cariboo, 1865
Watercolour, 9½" x 6¾"

PLATE 21
Edward M. Richardson
Williams Lake Indians, 1864
Watercolour, 5" x 5¾"

PLATE 22
R.G. Schofield
Antler Creek, Cariboo, March 1863
Watercolour, 7¼" x 9"

PLATE 23
R.G. Schofield
The Bald Mountain, Cariboo, March 1863
Watercolour, 7¼" x 9"

PLATE 24
Emily Carr
Gitwangak, Queen Charlotte Islands, 1912
Oil on canvas, 33" x 34¾"

PLATE 25
James W. Morrice
A Brittany Girl, c.1902
Pencil drawing, 6¾" x 4½"

PLATE 26
William Berczy
Portrait of a Nobleman, c.1785
Oil on paper, 4" circular

PLATE 27
Frederick A. Verner
A Young Indian Chief, 1871
Oil on canvas, 37" x 28"

PLATE 28
Frederick A. Verner
The Sentinel, 1874
Grisaille, 15½" x 27¼"

PLATE 29
Charles J. Way
View of Quebec from the River Marshes, c.1880
Watercolour, 11" x 20"

PLATE 30
F. McGillivray Knowles
A Quiet Ontario Village, 1897
Watercolour, 12" x 18"

PLATE 31
J.B. Wilkinson
Icebound on the St. Lawrence, 1878
Watercolour, 7½" x 10¾"

PLATE 32
Henry Sandham
Lake Scene with Mountains, c.1880
Watercolour, 13½" x 19"

PLATE 33
J.M. Barnsley
An East Coast Fishing Village, 1889
Watercolour, 11¼" x 16"

PLATE 34
Frederic M. Bell-Smith
A Thames Bridge, London, c.1897
Watercolour, 10" x 14"

PLATE 35
Frederic M. Bell-Smith
A Camp in the Rockies, 1889
Watercolour, 10¾" x 18¼"

PLATE 36
Edward Roper
A North West Coast Indian Village, c.1880
Oil on board, 12¼" x 20¼"

PLATE 37
Daniel Fowler
Landscape, Amherst Island, 1887
Watercolour, 12½" x 18½"

PLATE 38
Daniel Fowler
Game Birds – Still Life, 1869
Watercolour, 19" x 27"

PLATE 39
William Armstrong
*Squaw Plucking Ducks Near Fort William,
Lake Superior,* 1865
Watercolour, 6" x 9"

PLATE 40
William Armstrong
Indians in War Canoes, 1877
Oil on canvas, 8" x 12"

PLATE 41
Blair Bruce
A Summer Day in Normandy, c.1890
Oil on canvas, 30" x 59"

206

PLATE 42
Homer Watson
A Passing Storm, Doon, 1885
Oil on canvas, 24″ x 36″

PLATE 43
Lucius R. O'Brien
Fishing Near the Ottawa River, 1875
Watercolour, 9¾″ x 14″

PLATE 44
LeMoine FitzGerald
A Farm at Snowflake, Manitoba, c.1930
Oil on canvas, 7¼″ x 9⅛″

PLATE 45
Frederick H. Varley
A Flanders Battlefield, 1918
Watercolour, 7″ x 10″

PLATE 46
Frank H. Johnston
*The Lake at Hubert, 96 Miles North of
Sault Ste. Marie,* September 1918
Tempera on board, 16″ x 15½″

PLATE 47
David B. Milne
Two Maples, Palgrave, 1932
Oil on canvas, 18″ x 24″

PLATE 48
Lawren Harris
The Ramparts, B.C., c.1924
Oil on panel, 10½″ x 13¾″

PLATE 49
André Lapine
Captain Millar's Cottage, Lake Simcoe, 1933
Oil on panel, 15½″ x 11½″

PLATE 50
Horatio Walker
Hauling Firewood, Isle of Orleans, 1912
Oil on canvas, 28″ x 38″

PLATE 51
Albert Robinson
Malbaie, Quebec, 1927
Oil on panel, 11¼″ x 13″

PLATE 52
J.E.H. MacDonald
Cliffs Near Hubert, Montreal River, Algoma,
1919
Oil on board, 8½″ x 10½″

PLATE 53
Frederick H. Brigden
Valley on the Don River, c.1940
Watercolour, 11″ x 14″

PLATE 54
Manly MacDonald
Hauling Wood, Near Point Anne, Ontario,
c.1940
Oil on canvas, 20″ x 26″

PLATE 55
Franklin Carmichael
Autumn in the Northland, 1921
Oil on canvas, 30″ x 36″

PLATE 56
Clarence Gagnon
Une rue de Baie St. Paul, c.1923
Oil on panel, 6¼″ x 9¼″

PLATE 57
Tom Thomson
Pink Birches, Spring, c.1916
Oil on panel, 10½″ x 8½″

PLATE 58
Maurice Cullen
Cutting Ice, Sillery Cove, c.1912
Oil on canvas, 30″ x 40″

PLATE 59
Maurice Cullen
Spring Break-up, Cache River, c.1914
Oil on canvas, 18″ x 22″

PLATE 60
Robert Pilot
Late Winter, Perth, Ontario, 1930
Oil on panel, 12″ x 16¾″

PLATE 61
J.W. Beatty
Autumn, Algonquin Park, c.1915
Oil on canvas, 30″ x 38″

PLATE 62
Paraskeva Clark
Still Life with Fruit, c.1935
Oil on canvas, 27″ x 30″

PLATE 63
Arthur Lismer
Rapids, Algoma, 1924
Oil on panel, 9″ x 12″

PLATE 64
Arthur Lismer
Little Islands, MacGregor Bay, 1929
Oil on panel, 13" x 16"

PLATE 65
Frederick H. Varley
Summer in the Arctic, c.1937
Oil on canvas, 34" x 40"

PLATE 66
A.Y. Jackson
The St. Lawrence at St. Fidèle, c.1928
Oil on panel, 8½" x 10½"

PLATE 67
Paul Peel
Femme au Jardin, 1889
Oil on canvas, 30" x 25"

PLATE 68
James W. Morrice
The Market Place, St. Malo, c.1902
Oil on panel, 9¾" x 7"

PLATE 69
Tom Thomson
Spring Ice and Birches, c.1916
Oil on panel, 8½" x 10½"

PLATE 70
J.E.H. MacDonald
Pump and Pumpkins – A Sunny Corner, 1916
Oil on board, 8" x 10"

PLATE 71
Lawren Harris
Trees and Hill, Algoma, 1919
Oil on panel, 10¼" x 13½"

PLATE 72
David B. Milne
Across from the Garage, Palgrave, 1930
Oil on canvas, 16" x 20"

PLATE 73
Cornelius Krieghoff
The Habitant Peddler, c.1860
Oil on canvas, 11" x 9"

PLATE 74
Paul Kane
Buffalo Grazing, Indian Summer
Near Fort Carlton, c.1846
Oil on paper, 8¼" x 13¾"

PLATE 75
A.Y. Jackson
A Quebec Village, c.1929
Oil on panel, 8½" x 10½"

PLATE 76
Emily Carr
The Red Stump, c.1934
Oil on canvas, 25½" x 16½"

PLATE 77
Paul-Emile Borduas
Légers Vestiges d'Autumn, 1956
Oil on canvas, 25" x 32"

Index

213

This book was designed by Bob Young.